# An Invincible Spirit

T0303373

# An Invincible Spirit
## The Story of Don Fulk

## As Signed to Janet Allen

Gallaudet University Press
Washington, DC

Gallaudet University Press
Washington, DC 20002
http://gupress.gallaudet.edu

Library of Congress Cataloging-in-Publication Data

Names: Fulk, Don, 1942-1998, author. | Allen, Janet (Janet Anne), 1958-
    author.
Title: An invincible spirit : the Don Fulk story / [as signed to] Janet Allen.
Description: Washington, DC : Gallaudet University Press, [2019] | "Fulk is
    telling his own story, but it's 'as told to' Allen" --Email from publisher.
Identifiers: LCCN 2018042813| ISBN 9781944838478 (pbk.) |
    ISBN 9781944838485
    (ebk.)
Subjects: LCSH: Fulk, Don, 1942-1998. | Deaf--United States--Biography. |
    Quadriplegics--United States--Biography. | Deaf--Institutional
    care--United States. | Quadriplegics--Rehabilitation--United States.
Classification: LCC HV2534 .F85 2019 | DDC 305.9/08092 [B] --dc23
LC record available at https://lccn.loc.gov/2018042813

For Woody Osburn, who lived his life with courage and dedication to others.

A special Thank You to
Chase Chambers, for technical assistance with this book. Chase is a Tulsa University graduate, a freelance filmmaker, and the 2016 College Awards winner for the film *Deaf Code*.

# Contents

# PROLOGUE

Don Fulk passed away on February 4, 1998. I received the news of my good friend's passing around two o'clock in the morning. The phone rang, waking me from a deep sleep. When I picked it up, I heard the distinct sound of a telecommunications device for the deaf (TDD or TTY) on the other end. I groped in the darkness for my TTY, placed the receiver on it and typed HELLO GA (go ahead). Immediately Betty typed back that her beloved Don was gone. I sat on my bed and cried. Not so much for Don, because he was free of his wheelchair, but for me, because I would miss him.

I met Don in 1981 when I was working at the Tulsa Speech and Hearing Association as a secretary/sign language interpreter. One day, we received a frantic call. The TTY in our office was a monstrous, gray device that sat by my desk and made a great, rattling noise when it rang. It had a roll of paper that printed what the person on the other end of the line typed. That day, the message read, "Help, I am stuck in my house." Our director, Don Hastings, went to help and found Don Fulk unable to open the door. Don was so happy to receive our assistance that he became a regular visitor to our office. I began to understand his unique way of communicating and to look forward to his visits.

Don wanted his story told and asked me to write it down. I told him I would try my best. This was the beginning of decades of a remarkable friendship and a remarkable story. Don's apartment was not far from my house, and he would often visit. He couldn't get up the three steps into my house, so we sat out in the front yard in all kinds of weather. In summers, when it was hot, he would ask that I pour a tall pitcher of cold water on his head to cool him off. He would laugh that wonderful laugh of his every time and ask for more.

We would sit for hours; me cross-legged in the grass, writing furiously on mountains of yellow pads of paper spread across the yard, while Don signed laboriously, lifting his half-paralyzed arms as high as he could, moving his frozen fists in the air, telling stories from countless memories. I promised him I would finish his book one day. This is the fulfillment of that promise.

Don told me he felt it was important that others know about his experiences growing up deaf and, at age eighteen, becoming a quadriplegic, which compounded his challenges. Don had three dreams: to become independent, employed, and married. He achieved all three and much more. The stories he told me were filled with courage, determination, and inner strength, as well as humor and grace. His tenacity and patience showed in every story he told. Don possessed a sweet, yet dogged, determination to make things right, not only for himself but for others who face the same challenges.

I want to thank all of Don's family members who have assisted me with this effort: Kendall Fulk, Laurie Kimball, Steven Fulk, Val Kendall, and Kathy Douglas.

I want to also thank Larry Bishop, Chuck Laenger, Kirby Hodges, Carla Lawson, Janelle Hankinson, Doyle Dye, Glenna Cooper, Kathy Stroyick, Tsianina and Roy Kinney, Leon Hoover, Roland Sykes, Dr. Perry Sanders, Sarah Kennedy, and my son Ryan Tedder.

A special thank you to Woody Osburn, Kathleen Kleinmann, Gerald Davis, and Connie Foster, who were there when Don needed them.

And most of all to Betty Anne Fulk and Chase Chambers, who made this book possible and who stuck by me all of these years. I love you both.

Don began this book himself, so I am finishing it now in his words, as he would have wanted it. It took me many years to finish it, but after I recently retired from teaching, I was finally able to give it the attention it deserved. I had the chance to interview family members and important people in Don's life, thoroughly research his experiences, and speak with everyone he touched in any way.

I am so inspired by Don's courage, wit, will, and positive spirit. When you read his story, I hope you will be as well.

Janet Allen

# An Invincible Spirit

# 1

## Keeping Up

My name is Don Fulk. I was born on February 17, 1942. When I was three years old, I contracted spinal meningitis, which left me profoundly deaf. When I was eighteen, I had a swimming accident and became a quadriplegic. This is my story.

Canals run like rivers in my small hometown of Colton, California. When I was eight years old, I often went with my brother, Paul Howard, and two neighbor boys to the canals, where we waded in the water and caught crawdads. We filled our buckets with the crawly little things and took them home. The neighbor boys' father cleaned them, keeping the tails, and throwing out the rest. I knew that the family cooked and ate them. I decided I would never go to their house for supper.

Wherever the other boys went, I followed—always behind. They discussed their various plans for adventure, but because I couldn't hear and talk, I was never really included in their decision making. I only followed, curious about where they were going and where they might lead me.

I remember once they came upon a canal in the midst of tall weeds. I was not far behind. The only means of crossing the canal was a wooden pole stretched between the banks, on which the boys lightly skipped across. I happily ran to catch up, but when I came upon the pole, I hesitated. The other boys waited on the far bank, gesturing to me to hurry up. They grew impatient and began disappearing into the weeds and bushes.

The only way I could cross was to get down on my hands and knees, grasp the pole with both hands, and slowly crawl across. My heart beat like the wings of a hummingbird, but I slowly and painstakingly inched my way along, reached the other side, and ran to catch up with the other boys. I didn't know then but later came to understand that my deafness affected my sense of balance.

Don on bicycle with brother.

We journeyed on and eventually came upon a bridge with a train track. We looked over the sides and saw some men on the ground. Some were asleep, and others were cooking over a small campfire. They spied us and suddenly began picking up rocks and hurling them at us. I guessed they didn't want us to bother them or the boys had said something to them that they didn't like.

In those days, I had lots of fun making and playing with homemade toys, such as slingshots, wooden guns with rubber bands cut from old inner tubes, and makeshift boxcars. I used to play outside a lot, without shoes or shirt, with an old discarded tire. I remember rolling the tire beside me as I walked through my neighborhood, past the old wood-frame houses lining the dirt road that stretched away before me.

Sometimes I helped the landlord fill bottles with homemade beer from a large wooden barrel in his secret cellar. I thought it tasted awful and added it to the list with the crawdads. We boys also spent many hours playing "war," taking sides and throwing stones at each other.

In these ways, I filled my silent days before we had television. But after the television came, for me it, too, was silent.

Sometimes my brother and I would walk together to a small town nearby to swim in the neighborhood pool, but most of the time I went alone. I loved to dive and search the bottom of the pool for stray bobby pins or lost pennies. Often I would bring a dime with me to the pool, flip it into the air, watch it sink through the water, and dive in after it. I did this over and over. But one time, I flipped the dime high into the air and watched in dismay as it disappeared into the top of a fat woman's bathing suit. As she dug it out from between her huge breasts, I quickly dived under the water in order to avoid embarrassment. I decided to let her have that dime, no questions asked.

One day later that spring, my parents began packing suitcases and food baskets and putting them into the car. What's going on here, I wondered. Where were we going?

I tried to ask, but no one understood my sounds or seemed to want to bother with me. Of course, I probably would not have understood if they tried to explain.

We all got into the car and drove. And drove . . . and drove some more. It seemed an awfully long way, and I became quite bored. There was nothing for me to do except sit in silence and watch out the windows as the scenery grew increasingly monotonous. After two whole days, we arrived at somebody's house somewhere. We entered and I stared as my family hugged some people, and everybody started moving their mouths, seemingly all at the same time. I knew they must be nice people because they all smiled a lot, and they even hugged and kissed me, but I had no idea who they were. I found out years later that we were in Terre Haute, Indiana, and these people were my grandparents and aunts and uncles.

Back in California, we lived in a small house we rented from the family who lived behind us. We shared a backyard full of chickens, with a vegetable garden, and cornstalks. The landlord's sons used to play with Paul Howard. They built a secret clubhouse, using a hole in the ground about four feet deep and ten feet square. They made a roof with cardboard boxes and covered it with tree branches. They would go inside and conduct their secret business.

I longed to go in with them, but they never let me. One day I got so frustrated and angry with them that I picked up a heavy log, lifted it high over my head, and heaved it at the roof of the club-house. The entire roof collapsed with a poof of dust, and before I could plan my next move, the boys began chasing me.

My mother was in the backyard hanging clothes on the line, and I ran for the protection of her skirt. The other boys' mother saw what happened and came out to speak to my mother. From behind her skirt, I could see their mouths moving at each other. Their mother soon left, and a few weeks later we moved to San Bernardino. I think their mother was angry that day, and I have often wondered if the move might have had something to do with me.

We moved to San Bernardino in 1952. I was ten years old and had never attended school. I think my parents didn't really know what to do with me. I didn't know how to relate to them, and I did not feel particularly close to them.

# 2

## Communication

That year, 1952, I had my first encounter with school. On the first day, before I left for school, I learned my first word. My father took me aside and wrote something on a piece of paper. It read D-O-N. He pointed to the paper and then to me. I could hardly hold back my excitement. I had an identity. I was Don.

My father took me outside to wait for the school bus, and he rode with me to school. I don't remember the name of the school, but it had one classroom, seven students, and one teacher. The other kids in the class stared at me because I was new. But I realized they were like me when I saw them talk to each other with their hands instead of with their mouths. They used simple home-made signs that I picked up quickly.

My first day was a busy one. Right away, the teacher worked with me on making sounds and words with my voice and say-ing the other students' names. After pointing at pictures or vari-ous objects, the teacher showed me how to place my tongue, teeth, and lips while pushing my breath through my vocal cords in an effort to produce the proper

Don's father with his three sons.

sounds for each word. The teacher and I also placed our hands on each other's throats, feeling for vibrations. She tried to teach me the song "Happy Birthday to You."

5

However, even as I started school and began learning language, communication was an increasingly frustrating and embarrassing problem. Once, I was playing outside with two boys who lived a few houses down the street. I noticed that it was getting dark, and I wanted so much to tell them that I wanted to play with them again the next day, but I couldn't. For a few moments, I struggled with the problem of how to communicate. My eyes came to rest on a long stick lying nearby on the ground. I picked it up and drew a picture of the sun in the dirt. I motioned to the picture in the dirt, then toward the sun setting in the sky. I moved my hand slowly down, down, down, to indicate the sun setting, then I pantomimed going to sleep, then waking up, and running out to play. The other kids stared at me in wonder. They thought I was crazy or, perhaps, pretending to be some kind of goofy Indian guide. They left me standing there. I walked home and went to bed, frustrated again.

On another occasion, my brother motioned for me to follow. I followed him all the way through shortcuts, past trees, over a river bridge, until we arrived in town. I followed as he crossed streets, though sometimes I feared for our safety. At one point I screamed when it looked like a truck would hit me at a traffic light. I didn't understand the meaning of traffic lights and only learned about them later from my lip-reading teacher. When we appeared to have reached our destination, I realized that my brother wanted something because he gave me a dollar and tried to tell me something, but I didn't understand what he wanted. Finally he gave up, took the bill back, and ran off to catch the bus. I was left standing there. I never did find out what he wanted of me.

I have always hated Thanksgiving because I felt more alone then than at any other time. It was a day when many people came to our house and talked and laughed, and we all sat at a big table to eat lots of food. Thanksgiving scared me. I couldn't communicate with anyone, and they didn't try to communicate with me. I would sit patiently at the table eating my food, every now and then glancing around at the happy faces, and feeling terribly alone. Mouths constantly moved—if they were not eating, they were talking.

I suddenly realized that I needed to go to the bathroom. I wanted to leave the table, but I was afraid. I wanted to ask my mother to be excused, but I had no words. I shifted in my chair, uncomfortable and frightened, until the inevitable happened. I waited patiently for the meal to end. When it did and I stood up from the table, the awful evidence was there on my pants and on the floor. I ran to the bathroom, hating Thanksgiving all the more.

Occasionally, communication was a simple thing. Some of us kids used to make parachutes out of a piece of cloth with strings attached to each corner and the other end of the strings attached to a heavy nut from some old bolt. We would fling the small things into the air and watch them float gracefully to the ground.

I watched them, wondering if I could fly like that. Suddenly I had an idea. What about using a big sheet? I figured that if a small cloth could carry a nut, why couldn't a much larger sheet carry another kind of nut—me. I ran home and got a sheet. My aim was to jump off the roof of the garage and float gracefully, like the smaller parachute, to the ground. I thought it would be great fun. Halfway to the door, though, my mom caught me. She grabbed the sheet and looked at me sternly, her mouth moving, and her finger pointing. She had read my mind, and she foiled my plan.

Ever since I was very young, I have had vivid dreams and nightmares that I remembered as though they actually happened. One in particular that I still remember had to do with a butterfly. I wanted it so very much because it was the most beautiful butterfly I'd ever seen. I chased it everywhere until it landed on top of a huge flower. I snuck up on it, and when I tried to grab it, the flower's petals closed up with the butterfly still inside. I began peeling back the petals one by one, seemingly for hours and hours. With still more petals to go, thousands of bees suddenly came out of the flower and attacked me. I fought them off with my pillow. My mother quickly appeared at my bedside, helping me to calm down and go back to sleep.

Dreams such as these continued until I was in my thirties. Looking back, I wonder if my dreams had to do with the terrible frustration I felt and the loneliness and isolation of deafness. I think they might have had to do with my sitting at the dinner table night after night, head bowed, feigning an intense concentration on my food, eating quickly and silently while those around me engaged in happy conversation. I also think the dreams might have had something to do with my painful awareness of the impatience on the faces of my brothers and sisters and friends when I struggled to tell them, with guttural sounds and gesture, about things I saw or did. And I think, most of all, the dreams might have had to do with my longing to share deep personal feelings with my mother and father, only to have my efforts to do so stifled by fist-clenching frustration.

I could see that the sounds I made caused heads to turn and eyes to stare. I could see the concern on my mother's face when she heard my initial sounds. But after getting someone's attention, what could follow? I knew that I could think and feel and dream like anyone else. Thoughts, ideas, and feelings were there inside my head and my heart but the others didn't seem to know or understand this. In those early years, I didn't know how to tell them. I was so often filled with a sense of separation and bewilderment. Who was I, who are these people? Why am I different? How old am I? Where do I live? I had all these questions, but I didn't know the answers and had no way of getting them.

# 3

## The School for the Deaf

In 1954, when I was twelve, my parents sent me to the California School for the Deaf at Riverside, which was not very far from San Bernardino. I lived in a dormitory with other students my age. I began to learn things, in and out of the classroom. I began to learn that I would have to watch out for myself.

One of the first things I had to learn was how to get to school. My mother made the first trip with me by bus from San Bernardino to Riverside, but the next time I went home on a visit, she let me make the return trip alone. I arrived in Riverside, but I didn't know the name of the bus to take from the station to the school, ten miles away. I still could not write, so I couldn't ask anyone. I started walking. I didn't know the name of the street, but I knew the general direction, and I knew the school was on a hill. I walked and walked, even climbing trees to scan the horizon. Finally I spotted the hill and became so excited that I ran the rest of the way. Before I entered the campus, however, I sat down on a rock and rested for a long time. Then I noticed the sun was beginning to set, and I thought, I better hurry or I will be late for supper. I was relieved that I had made it.

I also learned that there would be boys like King. While outside playing with the other deaf boys, I noticed one boy with bronze skin and a duck-tail hairdo who seemed to be the leader of all things. He strutted around like he owned everything and every-one. His real name was Victor, but I decided to call him King.

One time our housemother, who was sixty years old and also deaf, appeared at the doorway with a huge bowl of popcorn.

Almost before I could blink my eyes, the boys charged her, with King in the lead. Popcorn flew in the air, as she took off, leaving it all behind. I believe she was genuinely frightened. The boys continued to push, shove, and fight to get that popcorn. All I could do was stare in shock. They looked like a bunch of animals. I stood and watched until there was nothing left outside the door but a shattered bowl.

Some mornings at five o'clock, King, who slept in another room, would saunter into the room where several boys and I slept and start turning beds upside down to jolt us out of our sleep, and he would persuade us to help with one of his schemes. Everyone was afraid of him, and although we wanted desperately to go back to sleep, most of us would readily agree to get up and help him with his little game. He didn't worry about anyone hearing the ruckus because the house parents were just as deaf as the boys. Since I didn't have sign language skills on par with the other boys, I was able to stay out of King's circle, so I usually ignored him and went back to sleep.

I was not afraid of King, and I let everyone know this. Word got around to him, which made him angry and he began continually challenging me. Once, he took half an orange, rubbed it in my face, and sprayed it on the walls of my room so I would be responsible for cleaning it up. He tried my patience one too many times, and I pushed him. Surprise spread across his face, and he came back at me. The other boys gathered round, curious to see who would win. Before we could determine a winner, though, one boy waved frantically at us to warn us that the housefather was coming, sure that he would punish us. When the housefather arrived, he asked what was happening.

King and I both replied, "Nothing," and the incident passed. But after that, King left me alone. I think he simply faced facts: I was bigger than he was, I was strong, and I was not afraid of him.

One day I saw an awful scene. One student was mentally challenged, and a bunch of the other boys made fun of him. About eight o'clock one night, four of the boys walked into my room, this boy following, on their orders. They formed a circle around him, laughing and signing fast. I didn't get all that was said. Then they opened their pajamas and urinated on him until his pajamas were soaked. The confused boy stood there, flinching, and I stood there, watching. I couldn't believe what I was seeing.

When the boys had their fill of "fun and games," they forced the poor boy to clean the floor. Then he slowly stood up, his face contorted, and left the room. The other boys laughed and talked about the fun they had. I turned away to go back to my bed and do my homework, but it bothered me. I felt upset and outraged because I had felt helpless to do anything about it. Those boys were at a higher level than I, and they could communicate more quickly and easily with each other. I knew that I should stay out of it, and I felt that it was not my place to say or do anything.

I thought, "When will it be my place?"

I was also learning things in the classroom. I started learning sign language every day from the other kids. My roommate, especially, was a huge help. Now that I was around sign language all the time now, I was picking it up fast. About the time I turned thirteen, I learned the days, weeks, and years, and how to tell time. I learned numbers and how to add and subtract. But I still didn't know how to write, so the teacher would sometimes write letters on the blackboard for me to copy and mail to my parents. I was fascinated to discover the names and amounts of coins. Here was the penny, the nickel, the dime, and so on. How wonderful to be able to recognize them and to know their value! Before, I could only lay down a bunch of coins on the counter and let the salesperson take his pick, and trustingly accept whatever change he offered. Now, I hoped I would be able to sell newspapers on the street.

Paul Howard soon began to learn to fingerspell, forming the letters of the alphabet on his hands in order to spell words. But it was several years before my parents learned any sign language. My father eventually learned to fingerspell. So did my mother, and she learned a few signs.

The autumn before I turned thirteen, I moved into the "Upper 111" dormitory. Dorms were assigned according to age groups. I was at the age where I started copying other boys' style of dress and their duck-tail hairdos. My hair looked like wax. I wore my collar upturned and my trousers low around my hips. With my penny loafers (with fringe), I thought I was cool and was sure that my new image would help me become more accepted by the others.

One night, something rather interesting happened. Around midnight, one of the boys tapped on my shoulder to wake me up.

I looked up and moved my hand in the sign for "what?"

He put his finger across his lips and gestured for me to follow him. We crept down the hallway in the dark and sat down on the floor with some other boys. I asked again and again, but they cautioned me to be quiet. Then one of the other boys opened a magazine and turned on a flashlight. The boys anxiously gathered round to look closer. In the glow of the flashlight, I saw that the title of the magazine was "Playboy." When I saw what was inside, I felt strange. I was shocked to see a woman's large breasts confronting me from the pages. I was confused and unsure—things were not as I thought.

"Where is her penis," I asked.

The boys looked at me and grinned.

"They don't have a penis, silly," one of them said.

This was a surprise to me. I just stared at the pictures and wondered, while I gawked. Suddenly a beam from another flashlight appeared down the hall. We all jumped up and ran to our beds, one boy taking the magazine with him, while a man with a big ring of keys on his belt passed by without noticing anything.

Back in my bed, panting from my run and staring into the darkness, I began thinking about the pictures, about the differences between men and women, and about where I had come from. I had always thought that I came from a basket. I had seen the cartoons. The baby kittens were always in baskets; the stork always brought the baby in a basket. Now, from what I understood of the boys' fast signing in the dark hallway, they were telling me that the basket story was not true. I was totally confused. I felt pressure in my mind to solve this problem. But sleep overcame me, and I did not solve it that night.

One day in school, they showed a picture of a family tree. I looked and studied all the branches coming out, going this way and that. There were the words "aunt" and "uncle," foreign and without meaning. And I became even more confused.

I played a lot of football in the years I was at the school. One day, our football coach told us we would get uniforms. I was very excited because we had not had any uniforms before. That night I had another dream. I vividly remember playing a thrilling game of football. Somehow, during that dream, I got up out of bed and hit my head against the wall. I blacked out and fell back on the bed. When the housemother arrived to wake us up for breakfast, she had to help me up. I had a very large bump on my head. Too bad I didn't have my helmet in time for the dream. I never did get to wear my football uniform. My family and I moved away before the team played its first game with uniforms.

# 4

## Oklahoma

In February 1956, when I was about to turn fourteen, we moved to Oklahoma. My parents had been separated for about a year—I was not sure why—and my father took a job as a linotype operator for an Oklahoma City newspaper. He returned to San Bernardino and one day showed up at the Riverside school. With his simple home-made signs, he communicated to me that we were moving, but he didn't say where. So I packed my clothes and sadly said goodbye to my friends.

When I saw my brother, he said, "Move to Oklahoma," and I wondered where that was. Everyone in the family piled into the car. I watched out the back window, the trailer rattling along behind as our house faded into the distance. I brought the road map with me and watched for road signs. I learned some of the names of the towns that we went through and was able to follow our progress to some extent. We seemed to be traveling into the mountains between New Mexico and Texas, and many of the city signs gave their elevation.

Somewhere along the way, we drove to the top of a mountain, where we stopped for gas, and then began the drive down the other side of the mountain. There were many long curves, and we were going faster and faster. My brother and I delighted in the extra speed; we thought it exciting and great fun.

Then I noticed my father was sweating and looked scared. My brother was not smiling anymore. Now he looked panicked, and he started screaming. My siblings stared with wide eyes, and they bounced in their seats, hanging onto each other, crying, and yelling. I was frightened, and I felt my throat clench with fear. I did not know my father had hit the brakes to slow the car, but the brakes were not working. Eventually he stopped the car, the trailer jackknifed, and the police came with their lights flashing. We all sighed with relief. My father traded in the car for another one, and we drove on. We arrived in Oklahoma City late one evening. The next day, we celebrated my fourteenth birthday and Paul Howard's sixteenth.

In April, I enrolled in fifth grade at the Oklahoma School for the Deaf, in Sulphur, approximately eighty-five miles southeast of Oklahoma City. For the next four years, I lived in a dormitory, while my family continued to live in Oklahoma City. Those years settled into the normal and natural routine of students away at school. I was only home for vacations and holidays.

Besides my older brother, Paul Howard, I had five younger siblings. My sister Val, who was twelve and a brown-haired beauty with a mind of her own, was the typical big sister who took care of everyone. Kendall was seven, tall, shy, but playful with blue-green eyes and dark hair. Next was Kathy, who was five. She had brown eyes and brown, curly, shoulder-length hair. She was shy and serious and a good student in school. She tended to be a tomboy and loved to play outside. Then there was Laurie, who was three and had brown hair and brown eyes. She was quiet around strangers, but when she got older and her friends came around, she could get loud really fast. When she became old enough to go to school, she struggled but was not one to give up. Last, but not least, Steven was the baby of the family. At this time, he was only one year old. He had hearing problems in one ear that later resolved. He was a sweet, shy, blue-eyed, brown-haired child that the others loved to hold. I loved to play with him too.

Even though I was able to teach my family some sign language and how to fingerspell, they soon forgot because I was away so much. Whenever I came home, communication with them was still awkward. I didn't feel very close to my family at all. But on the weekends, whenever I came home on the bus, my brothers and sisters always greeted me with a rush of excitement. They especially delighted in raiding my suitcase for any comic books I might have brought.

One time when I was home from school, Paul Howard and I went on an overnight fishing trip at Lake Texoma with Kendall. It was a fun and exciting trip out in the boat, just us, fishing part of the night and camping the rest of the night. We had a fright, though. Kendall, who was only about nine years old then, fell into a hole under the water, disappeared, and we thought he wasn't coming back up. He resurfaced quite a while later, but he was fine. On the way home, we stopped for hamburgers and they were really good.

Visits were infrequent, but always fun. On another visit home when I was sixteen, Kendall excitedly fingerspelled H-E-L-L-O to me with a huge grin on his face. I tousled his hair playfully and nodded, appreciating the effort.

During another visit, both of my little brothers snuck down the stairs when they were supposed to be in bed. I caught them out of the corner of my eye and, with the biggest yell I could muster, I charged up the stairs after them. It must have been loud, because their faces lit up with excitement and they jumped with astonishment as they turned and dashed back up the stairs, giggling and punching each other.

I remember one particular time, though, when my baby brother Steven was about four. I had placed him on my shoulders, and we were prancing happily about the room, or so I thought, but Steven was not happy.

I didn't know this until I detected a worried, anxious look from my mother and a shake of her head, saying, "No!"

When I put him down, I discovered that he was crying.

My mother had to explain to Steven, "Your brother cannot hear, he didn't know you were crying."

After that, I made sure I could always see him in a mirror.

❖

I loved comic books, but it was not until during my first year at the Oklahoma School for the Deaf that I began to get full enjoyment from them. A custodian at the school, who was also deaf, noticed that while I spent a lot of time looking at comic books, I only looked at the pictures and ignored the words.

He came to me one day, shook his head, and said, "No, Don."

He told me to read the words. Before that, I had no idea the words were important.

Nightmares continued to bother me at school, and sleepwalking became a problem. Two dreams remain vivid in my memory. In one, I wrestled with a huge and terrible snake, seemingly forever. When I woke up, I discovered that during the struggle I had left my bed. The next morning, another student wanted to know why I had "choked" his leg during the night.

In the other dream, I experienced a sensation of movement and found myself alone in a raft somewhere in the middle of the ocean. The sky was clear and the sun blazing hot, but the waves were rough and sharks were all around. I was too scared to move an inch, so I lay perfectly still for what seemed like many hours, until I became so very tired I fell asleep. When I awoke, I realized I was still in my bed. Every inch of my body was soaked with perspiration, as were the bed and pillow.

Sometimes my sleepwalking escapades created a considerable amount of confusion. There was a heavy wooden table, about nine feet long, in my bedroom. When sleepwalking one night, I saw a little green man at one end of the table. I stood at the other end of the table and, when the little green man moved to the left, I moved to the right, lifted the table up as high as I could, and threw it at him. I ran away while the table was still in the air.

When the table hit the floor, it caused vibrations strong enough to wake all the deaf boys on both the first and second floors. Because of my reputation for sleepwalking, the boys had an idea who had created the commotion and immediately began to look for me. Due to the vibrations from the falling table and the lights coming on from nearby rooms, I awoke and found myself in a hallway. After the boys vacated my room to search for me, I returned to bed, where they eventually found me.

On one occasion, the boys told me that about seven of them tried to restrain me while I was sleepwalking, but they were unable to hold me because I was so strong and powerful, more so than when I was awake. My dormmates suggested various remedies or controls, but we did not test most of them. One of the most absurd suggestions was that they tie my wrists to my bed before I went to sleep. Of course, I didn't care for that idea. We tried it, it hurt my wrists, and I couldn't sleep with such restrictions.

A male staff member at the school told my dormmates that pouring a pail of water on me while I was sleepwalking might cure me of the problem, and they decided to test this idea. The next time I sleepwalked, the boys came after me with a pail of water. What they didn't know was that at that moment I had awakened. I turned around and faced the boy carrying the pail. He became so frightened that he threw a few drops of water at my face and dropped the pail and ran. Later, he said I looked like I was going to kill him. I thought that was pretty funny.

One afternoon, all of us came close to having a real nightmare. As I walked from the bathroom to my bedroom, I did not see a single soul. I wondered where everyone had gone. I went outside and still encountered no one. I felt strange because the place looked like a ghost town. I sensed something must be wrong. I walked back inside the dormitory and discovered a large group of people huddled together on the first floor.

"What happened?" I asked.

They said, "Tornado!"

For some strange reason, everyone had been alerted except me. As soon as the danger passed, I ran to the top of the building and saw a huge black cloud. The tornado had missed us by only two miles.

A few hours later, my mother called our superintendent's wife and asked if I was safe. The superintendent's wife came and told me that my mother was the only mother who had called. Everyone teased me about it, but I felt that I had the best mother in the world. Who else would have put up with the T-shirt I muddied up from playing football that I brought home in my suitcase the weekend before the tornado?

When my mother took the shirt out of the suitcase, I saw her eyes say, "What in the world?"

During summers, holidays, and other times I was home, I worked as a busboy at an Italian restaurant in Oklahoma City. I also became quite interested in linotype, my father's line of work. The school had instruction on setting type; there was an old-fashioned machine where you took the letters from a drawer and arranged the type in a box. I became quite good at it and was considered best of all the boys in the class. My father was quite excited about my learning to be a linotype operator. He came to the school to see what we were doing, talked to the teacher, and started helping me learn as much as he could teach me. He mentioned that he might be able to help me find a job in Oklahoma City where I could use my new skills.

While at the Oklahoma School for the Deaf, I stayed busy with a lot of activities. I played quite a bit of basketball, ran track for two

The basketball team. Don is number fifty.

years, and played football the last season I was there, when I was seventeen. By that time I had grown to six feet, two inches, and weighed about two hundred pounds. My family would come from time to time and watch me play basketball. I think my brothers especially enjoyed watching their big brother play, and it made me proud to see them sitting in the bleachers clapping for me.

There were no swimming facilities or a swimming team at the school, but the school was located near Platt National Park, through which Travertine Creek ran. We swam in the creek when the weather was warm enough. The older students, sixteen, seventeen, and eighteen-year-olds, often went there when school was over for the day. I also developed an interest in chess and started learning how to play the game. I spent time with a classmate, a deaf girl who I considered my girlfriend for a while. We went to movies and restaurants, but we soon became no more than friends, and the relationship ended.

My eighteenth birthday passed in February. I completed my freshman year of high school and went home for a vacation.

# 5

## Forever Changed

Twilight Beach is in Bethany, a small town to the northwest of Oklahoma City, just outside the city and not far from where we lived. Twilight Beach was like a large swimming pool, but instead of concrete, it had a sandy bottom and sandy sides. A large circular hole had been gouged out of the earth and partially filled with sand before adding the water, in order to give the pool a beach-like appearance. Around portions of the bank and over the water's edge sat a sort of wooden ledge for diving. Also, in the center of the pool, there was a large wooden pier where swimmers could sit or from which they could dive into the deeper water surrounding it. The place was privately owned and operated and was staffed with lifeguards. It was completely fenced in, and we had to pay to enter. There were no picnic facilities, no trees, or picnic tables, so we would usually spread a blanket on the grass to eat there.

It was Father's Day, in June 1960. My parents, brothers, and sisters—the whole family—had planned an outing and a picnic supper at Twilight Beach. Paul Howard and I went together in his convertible. We arrived early because the rest of the family had gone to pick strawberries, and while we waited for the rest of the family to arrive, we decided to go swimming.

I was a good swimmer, and that afternoon I began diving from the bank in an area that I often dived from. Soon some pretty girls entered the water in front of me, so I moved over slightly where it was clearer for diving. I remember diving into the water, and then everything went black. Suddenly, through the blackness, I could see the white sand very clearly. It was not far from my face—I was floating face down in three feet of water. I tried to get up but couldn't. It felt like my head was floating around without my body. When I couldn't seem to hold my breath any longer, I saw a hand coming toward me. I thought it was Paul Howard's hand and was surprised to realize that it was mine, just floating. It was very strange. I couldn't understand what had happened to me.

Paul Howard was in the water near me and thought I was only playing dead, so he picked me up and threw me out into the water again. Then he realized that something was very wrong.

He and the lifeguard carried me to the bank and laid me out on an incline on the grass. They looked at me, their faces questioning. I mouthed that I could not move, but only Paul Howard knew what I was saying, and he explained to the lifeguard. They told me that I would be okay and to not worry. Out of the corner of my eyes, I saw people gather around and the ambulance, lights flashing, drive right onto the grass beside me.

The ambulance took me to the emergency room at Baptist Memorial Hospital in Oklahoma City. There, many doctors swarmed around me. One of them used a pin to see if I could feel any sensation, and it was some time before I realized that he was testing for feeling, much less that he was using a pin. I could not feel anything below a point about five inches beneath my chin. Initially, I had no sensation in my shoulders and arms, but in the weeks to follow, I regained feeling in my shoulders, the inside of my arms, and a portion of my hands.

The doctors determined that I had sustained fractures in my cervical—or neck—vertebrae. I had dislocated my spine at levels four, five, and seven of the cervical vertebrae, resulting in transection—a complete tearing—of the spinal cord. The break at the fifth cervical vertebrae was the most severe, while the breaks at the fourth and seventh were not quite as bad. These breaks resulted in permanent paralysis below a point high on my chest; below that level, I had no feeling, and nothing could be done to restore my ability to move muscles below this point. Fortunately, other functions, such as digestion, circulation, and glandular responses, can operate independently of the spinal cord.

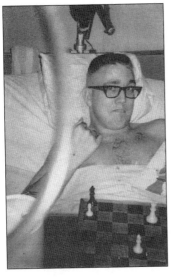

Don in the hospital bed.

Due to the location of the fractures, I could still control the flexor muscles in my arms and thankfully regained use of them. Doctors told me that if the transection had occurred a fraction of an inch higher, I wouldn't have been able to breathe outside an iron lung. They also told me that the mortality rate for this type of injury was very high.

As soon as the doctors concluded their preliminary tests, evaluations, and diagnoses, they began treating my injury. First, they shaved all the hair off my head. They found a large swollen spot on the top of my head, which was probably caused by hitting my head during the dive. The doctors gave me a shot to put me to sleep and wheeled me away to the x-ray room. I woke up and found myself in a Stryker frame, which would be my home for the next six months.

A Stryker frame is a large metal structure used instead of a bed and which enables the patient to be turned regularly—this is critical for a quadriplegic, in order to prevent or minimize the occurrence of bedsores. Between the sides of the frame stretches a layer of canvas covered with a thin layer of foam, on which the patient lies. When it is time to turn the patient, an attendant covers the patient with a second, similar frame. The patient is literally tightly sandwiched between the two frames with straps and then turned by hand with the aid of a kind of axle supporting the frame at both head and foot. The structure keeps the body rigid and in place throughout the turn. After the turn is completed, the patient lies on the newly installed frame, and the attendant removes the straps and the first frame. When the patient is in the stomach-down position, a grill-like device that looks like a catcher's mask covers the face, and strips of soft padding support the forehead and chin. Mirrors strategically placed on the floor enable the patient to see whatever is happening around him and whoever is talking to him. In my case, it was imperative that my neck be kept absolutely straight. Doctors drilled a hole into each side of my skull, into which they inserted an attachment resembling a pair of ice tongs. They hooked this up to a pulley and rope, to which they attached thirty-five pounds of iron weights. The weight was enough to keep my head pulled straight. I must have looked like Frankenstein.

Back at Twilight Beach, when my family arrived at the entrance gate, the pool employees stopped them and gave them the tragic news.*

My mother immediately began to cry, and my sister remembers her saying, "Why couldn't it have been Paul Howard?"

At first, my sister thought it was a horrible thing to say but then realized that, in the shock of the moment, all our mother could think about was that I was already deaf and it just did not seem fair. I know some people thought I would have been better off if I had died. In fact, shortly after I entered the hospital, some deaf men from Arkansas or Missouri came to visit me, apparently just to see what I looked like.

"You're going to die next month, I guess," one of them said to me. I laughed, because I considered the remark so absurd.

A couple of years later, when a couple of deaf neighbors came to visit me, they approached me with an obvious attitude of pity and remorse. I did not feel comfortable the whole time they were there. As they were leaving, one of them lingered behind.

---

* My father sued the owners of Twilight Beach. After a court battle that lasted two years, he eventually received a settlement of $10,000. Shortly after that, the swimming facility closed.

"Do you want me to go and bring you a gun, so that you can end all your suffering?" he asked me.

I was shocked. "No, thank you," I replied, "I'm thankful that I'm still alive."

❖

At the hospital, my parents stood over me, anxiously asking how I felt. My mother asked if I would be more comfortable in a regular bed. She didn't realize the importance of keeping me where I could be turned often. Common problems quadriplegics experience that result from immobility include bedsores, kidney stones, and issues with circulation and elimination.

Mine was not a common type of injury, which meant the Stryker was very rarely used at the hospital, and the doctors and staff were not very experienced with it. Understandably, perhaps, complications arose. Of course, some staff were more experienced than others, but twice the orderlies forgot to lock the bolt before turning the frame, and the frame fell down while my head was still hooked up to the weight pulley system, causing the tongs to tear loose and blood to run down my face.

The first time this happened, the doctor had to drill two new holes into the sides of my head. The second time, he had to drill a hole on the top of my head. A few other times when nurses were rushed, shifts were changing, and, once, when the doctor himself was careless, I was allowed to slip or fall, but the consequences were less serious. It wasn't long before a bedsore suddenly appeared and they realized they needed to turn me more frequently.

Occasionally, I had involuntary muscle spasms that caused me to shift into awkward positions. Once, a contraction in my legs was so strong I fell out of the frame. The force of the spasm threw me so far out of position that the weight of my body pulled me out of the frame and onto the floor. The nurse could not figure out how I could have gotten into such a fix, and she even scolded me for it, thinking I had done it on purpose. Fortunately, the tongs were no longer in my head when this happened. The doctor had removed them after about three months. I stayed in the Stryker frame for about six months, but during the last several weeks I was in a more sophisticated, electronically operated model. It rotated about in a circle, giving a wide variety of angles and positions. I liked it, but life in the frame was still pretty restricted.

Once again, I found myself with the problem of communication. It was very difficult to talk to the nurses because, at first, both of my hands and arms were paralyzed. I couldn't write, use sign language, or even gesture. I had to mouth everything I wanted to say, mostly one letter at a time, and only a few words like "water," "TV," or "hot." It was not easy. It was difficult even just to get someone to scratch my neck. One day during the second month after the accident, while I was still in the Stryker frame, my father was standing by the bed when the back of my neck began to itch something terrible. I twisted my face and wiggled my eyebrows to let him know something was wrong.

"What is it?" my father asked.

I nodded my head to one side repeatedly and blinked my eyes and rolled them to the side; I curled my mouth down, grimaced, and contorted my face. Finally, when I wrinkled my nose as if I was about to sneeze, he understood.

"An itch," he said.

I nodded frantically.

He asked, "Where?"

Again, I nodded my head and rolled my eyes to the side.

"There?" I shook my head.

"There?" he asked again.

Still not right, so I shook my head again.

The itch was getting worse and my eyes were beginning to water, but at last my father's hand hit the right place, and the relief was wonderful. Days went by and the itching became worse and worse; the doctor told my father that it meant my neck was healing inside. About four months into my stay at the hospital, I began to

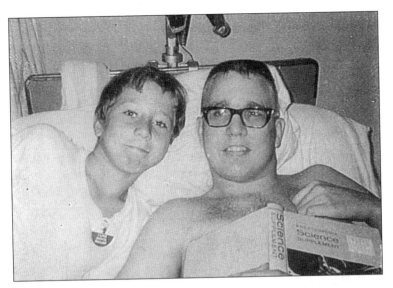

Don in the hospital with family.

develop a technique for writing messages with a pencil clenched between my teeth. I would use this technique for the rest of my life.

In September, physical therapy began. The nurse started making me exercise my arms, hands, and fingers. It hurt terribly, but of course it was absolutely necessary and good for my muscles. In spite of the pain, the therapist made me keep working.

She was a real character and kept saying things like, "I love to see you tortured! I enjoy every minute of it!"

After about two weeks, I started to control my arms again, and only certain parts were still weak. I kept exercising, and little by little, my arms became strong again. Therapy always began with the arms first, then the legs, because the arms were more important. The therapist worked with my legs later, but they did not respond. The therapy helped keep the leg muscles toned but did not do much to help me use them again. My leg muscles have long since become stiff and thin.

For the therapy sessions, an attendant would remove me from the Stryker frame, put me in a wheelchair, and take me to the therapy room. After therapy, I would return to the frame. I was forced to learn to push my own wheelchair.

My father kept wanting to push me, but the attendant would say, "No, Don needs to push it for himself."

Since I could not pull on the wheels themselves to move the wheelchair, I used a chair that had knobs on the wheels that I could grab and push myself. It was very tiring. When they first tried to put me in the wheelchair, I would black out because I had been lying down so long it had affected my circulation. Later on, I started sweating a lot and having chills. Every time I used the wheelchair, I would always experience so much sweating, followed by chills. I never felt comfortable in the wheelchair. Everyone, including the doctors, told me that I was only afraid and that I worried too much. I tried to tell them that I was not worried nor afraid, but no one would listen.

Perhaps the best part of the therapy sessions was the special whirlpool bath. I enjoyed the time in the whirlpool very much— that is, when the nurses were able to keep me from sliding down in the water and nearly drowning.

I mentioned the violent leg contractions that, on one occasion, threw me off the Stryker frame. Muscle spasms became a common occurrence—even a problem. But as I understand it, they had a beneficial effect in that they made the muscles work. One of the first spasms I had caused me to move my toes, and an orderly called my mother and father over to see.

When they pointed it out to the doctor, he said, "Just a spasm. Doesn't mean that he will walk again."

I understood that some of the spasms were caused by kidney stones passing through the penis. The spasms got worse, causing my legs to flip in the air and making it difficult to get me into bed or a wheelchair. Once, while a nurse was giving me a bath, I inadvertently kicked her in the chin. It made her mad. She thought I had done it on purpose. Eventually, the doctor suggested they do something to put the spasms to an end, to which my father agreed, so the doctor performed an operation on my back. It has subsequently been acknowledged that the operation should never have been performed.

When I could get up in the wheelchair and move my arms, someone would always bring me some food, but I got tired of people feeding me all the time. I thought things would go better if I could do it for myself. So they started bringing me fixings for a sandwich on a tray, but I couldn't hold things together too well and it usually turned out to be a mess, which discouraged me.

One day, I was hungry and really wanted to make and eat my own sandwich. I wanted a really big one with everything on it, and I worked excitedly—though awkwardly—to assemble it. At last, I raised the sandwich to my mouth and bit down hard. My teeth struck something hard. I thought the meat must be unusually tough, so I tried again. Again I bit down on something hard. I tried different spots, without luck, until suddenly the sandwich seemed to jump at me and I realized it was my hand I had been trying to bite. I chuckled because I only had a little bit of feeling in the fingers near the thumb area and knew I had bitten myself only because of the jerk of my hand from a muscle spasm. At the end of about five months—about when I left Baptist Memorial Hospital—my appetite began to improve and I was able to eat.

Another common complaint of quadriplegics is boredom. Except for the regular hospital room routine, the occasional flash of pictures on the television—when I was in a position to see it—and the occasional visitor, it was just the silence. And the immobility. It was virtually impossible to read in the frame.

One of the teachers from the school for the deaf volunteered to come and help take care of me at no charge. She came every now and then, and it was very nice. She helped a lot. She was somebody I could communicate with, and she would interpret what the nurses said and what was being said on the television. My mother called the school and welcomed my friends to come and visit me at the hospital. One day in October, a whole busload of students showed up. They were in town for the State Fair and came by to cheer me up. I appreciated it. But some days no one came.

I remember one particular day when no one had been in to see me all day, and nothing was going on. I wanted to see somebody, anybody. Loneliness filled the air, and I felt I would go crazy if I had to stare at the walls one more minute. I had to do something, so I did a rather childish thing. My gaze settled on the I.V. in my arm. Suddenly, I yanked it out with the little movement I had in my arm. A shadow quickly appeared at the door and an angry nurse approached my bed. Her lips gave me a good talking to, and for a moment I was glad I was deaf so I couldn't hear her words. I just smiled at her angry face. Someone was there.

I left the hospital in November. I had been there five months. It was too expensive for me to remain there any longer. There was a special nurse who came to help me at the hospital for a time. Deaf people from all over the state of Oklahoma had helped pay for my services, but the money had long since run out. The government would help pay for my care at the children's hospital, and so in November I moved into the Children's Convalescent Center in Bethany.

Although many difficult years and trying times followed, I always felt that my life had been spared because of God's plans for me, and I hoped that someday I would know what those plans were. Mixed with all the disappointments and tribulations, I was always able to find varying amounts of hope, a little bit of happiness, and a lot of acceptance.

# 6

## Soul Searching

I was amazed to see so many babies with health problems at the Children's Convalescent Center. Some had muscle problems or nervous disorders, others had large heads on small bodies. I was in a new world now. I had never been exposed to all the frailties and physical disorders that children might have. I shared a room with eight kids. They played rough, jumping on the beds and wrestling with each other. It was an interesting sight to see the little kids in their little wheelchairs zooming down the hall in a do-or-die race.

One day, one kid, perhaps ten years old, sat on his bed in our room studying his homework. He shifted around, not comfortable, until he suddenly and deliberately lifted each of his legs and wrapped them around the back of his neck. How curious, I thought, he must have a rubber body! Perhaps I was struck with the sight of what, for me, was such an impossibility.

I taught a few of the kids a few signs and a limited amount of fingerspelling. I guess I sort of became one of the kids and felt insulted if I wasn't always included in their activities.

One day, an orderly came into the room and made what was apparently an announcement; all the kids jumped up and ran out of the room. I motioned for him to come to my bed and tell me where everyone went. He wrote a note saying that they had gone to the doctor for check-ups, and then he left. About two and a half hours later, the kids came back, running and jumping. One little boy, who I was able to lip-read pretty well, came up to me and asked why I didn't go to the movie with them. I let out a scream of shock when I found out that they had not gone to the doctor after all!

Another boy of about thirteen came to my side. I grabbed his fingers and formed them into the letters L-I-E. He could understand fingerspelling and immediately asked me to make the sign. I showed him with a brush of the hand under the chin.

"I lied?" he asked.

I pointed in the direction the orderly had gone, and he knew who I meant.

"I'll go get him," he said, and left.

A moment later, he was back, saying that the man had refused to come.

"So what shall we do?" I asked.

By this time, all the kids were parading around yelling, "Lie," with their little hands flying in the sign for "Lie, lie, lie."

They were enjoying their newfound game.

I saw an R.N. approaching; she had apparently heard the game. She found out what had happened and called the staff together around my bed.

She handed me a note that read: "We are sorry, we will be sure to take you to the movie next time."

Then each of the staff offered their hand to shake mine, but I refused to let the orderly shake my hand. I guess that wasn't very nice, but I was still disgusted with him and wanted him to know it.

It was at the Children's Convalescent Center that I finally came face to face with the realization that I would never walk again. In the early days at the hospital, I was filled with—and fed—a lot of optimism. Everyone was so encouraging about how things would work out in due time. The doctors kept saying that I would go back to school and back to playing football. I suppose they knew all along and were only trying to make me feel better, but at the time I believed them.

I always thought I would walk again, maybe the next week. I kept telling my family to hurry things along, to get the show back on the road, I wanted to walk. I wanted to play football; I wanted to get back to school. I suppose after a few months, I began to accept the situation to some extent, or I at least became resigned to the fact that it would take a long time. But after a month or so at the convalescent center, I had to face the certain truth that I would never walk again.

I was going to therapy sessions four times a week, and was trying to do a lot of intensive work with my wheelchair and my exercises. More therapy and more exercise, I thought, and I'll eventually walk again. In the room where I did my therapy, I often saw another young man, about twenty-one years old, who also had a broken neck. One day, he started to use braces on his legs, and the nurses were helping him with the adaptation. He was also using a type of crutches.

As I watched them help him to stand, I thought perhaps I would be able to do the same thing. I told the nurse that that was what I wanted to do.

She said, "No. It is too early for you to do that."

I kept asking her every day to let me try, and she kept saying no.

After I insisted, she explained to me that the other man's neck had been broken in a different place than mine, and I would not be able to do what he was able to do.

"Here, let me show you," she said.

She bent my arm up at the elbow, with my palm facing me, and held her finger pressed against the backside of my arm at the wrist. She asked me to push her finger away with my arm. I laughed, thinking how simple it would be for me to do that. But I couldn't. I couldn't move my arm down, much less push her finger away. I realized for the first time that I could not move my arm in that way. That in the past, the therapist had always moved it for me, or the force of gravity or some other weight had taken care of it. Without the strength or ability to use my arms in that way, I could not use crutches. I was shocked.

"I am sorry," the nurse said.

"Will I ever be able to do what the other guy is doing?" I asked.

"I really don't know," she said.

Still, with more therapy and enough exercise, I thought. A few days later, during a therapy session, I saw a woman doing the same kind of exercises I was doing. I could read the other woman's lips saying to me that I would never be able to walk again.

"Is it true," I asked the nurse, "that I will never be able to walk again?"

She nodded, "Yes, that is true. You will never walk again."

At that point, I knew it was a fact that I would have to accept. I suppose the nurse could have lost her job if the doctor found out what she told me.

After I was at the Convalescent Center for six weeks or so, I got rid of the Stryker frame and got a special hospital bed. It was then that I began to read to help pass the time. A special kind of table rolled over and hooked to the bed; it was ideal for holding a book or magazine, and I pushed at the pages to turn them.

The center had a library, and the occupational therapist would bring me books to read. I remember the first book the therapist brought me to read. I don't remember the name of it—something about a little boy and a baby elephant—but I found it very interesting. Reading for pleasure was not so bad.

When my brother came to visit one day, I was excited to report that I had finished the book. He took a look at the book and began to laugh. I asked him why, and he replied that it was a children's book, meant for a twelve-year-old. That really hit me hard and I began to realize how far behind I was compared to other boys my age. I decided that the least I could do was try to improve my reading skills. I began to check out books from the library constantly. I read *Perry Mason* and other detective stories. I pored through novels like *The Adventures of Tom Sawyer* and *The Adventures of Huckleberry Finn*. I also enjoyed *Reader's Digest, Science News,* and newspapers, and I tried to read the Bible. And of course I read, and was much impressed by, the well-publicized true story of *Joni,* a girl who also suffered with the problems of a broken neck.

I was soon reading an average of three books a week, a practice I kept up for many years. I hoped that this would help me increase my knowledge of the world that I wanted so much to be a part of. I was not able to return to the Oklahoma School for the Deaf. My picture appeared in the school yearbook for the year I would have graduated, but only as a dedicatory tribute.

During my time at the Convalescent Center, I had three main problems. They would persist for a long, long time before anyone was able to eventually solve them. The first problem was the intense sweating and chills that started in the hospital and continued to plague me. Every time I used the wheelchair, I experienced heavy sweating. It made my time in the wheelchair most uncomfortable. No one seemed to know of anything that could be done about it; they attributed it to physical strain and mental tension. Oddly enough, I did not sweat while lying in bed.

The second problem was really terrible skin ulcers, or bedsores. I had one on each hip that was as big as a saucer and that went all the way to the bone. The doctors were afraid they were too deep to heal. They suggested my legs be amputated, but that idea enraged my parents. We started a regimen in which I would stay on my stomach all night, turn over on my back about eight o'clock in the morning, and keep the sores covered with an ointment. After a year of this, the sores completely healed.

The third problem involved eliminating waste from the bladder and bowels. The urine collectors were always leaking and would come off about three times each day. I found that this kind of problem would be hard to control and would last a long time.

The time came when my parents wanted to take me home to stay with them. They thought they would be able to take care of me without too much difficulty. I had been at the Convalescent Center for a little over a year. It was now December 1961, and I moved home just before Christmas. Things seemed to work out satisfactorily, and I lived at my parents' house on 34th Street for two years, from 1961 to 1963.

There was still so much discomfort and messiness connected with the wheelchair—the ever-recurring sweating and the difficulty with keeping the waste collectors connected—that it seemed better to simply avoid the hassle. Consequently, I stayed in bed all the time.

Most of the work of caring for me fell to my mother because my father was gone from home so much, either at work or out of town. We had suspicions that there might be other reasons he was not around. My younger brothers and sisters were usually in school or otherwise occupied, and Paul Howard had gone away to the Air Force. Since I was in bed most of the time, there was not so much to be done for me, and my mother seemed to be able to handle it.

The room arrangement was more or less the same as at the center. I had a special hospital bed, and there was a trapeze-like bar suspended above it I could use to help lift the upper part of my body (I could use my arm muscles in that way). Therefore, with my help and the use of pillows and such, it was fairly easy for my mother to turn me as often as was necessary. The doctor had instructed her in the proper procedure before my parents brought me home.

I also had the special rolling table that held reading materials so conveniently. I read a lot, since it was one of the few things I could do. I had a bird to help keep me company—a blue parakeet, I suppose it was, named Polly who roamed freely around the room. Often, as I read a book, Polly would come from out of the covers of the bed, crawl up between the book and my face, and peck my nose and give me kisses. I guess Polly loved me; it was certainly a welcome source of diversion for me.

My brother, Kendall, came into my room one day and told me with signs, gestures, and writing that he had come home from school and saw our mother sitting in the living room crying, holding a wallet with money in it. He asked her what was wrong, and she replied that our father had left. Kendall told her that our father would probably be back and to not worry.

"No, he's done this before," she replied. "He is not coming back."

Kendall told me he thought our father may have had a gambling problem, but he wasn't sure. I had mixed emotions about our father leaving. I had never felt close to him. On the one hand, I felt relieved to be free of his temper tantrums and angry outbursts. He would often slap my brothers and sisters across the face or on the head if he was unhappy with something they said or did. I remember one time, my sister told me our father chased her up the stairs beating her with a hanger. We lived in constant fear of his rage. I didn't like the runny scrambled eggs that he brought in to me, but I was afraid to ask him to please cook them a little more. I would, instead, ask my sister to do it. He wasn't there often enough, thankfully, for me to have to deal with.

On the other hand, I felt bad that he was abandoning us and our mother, and I was unsure about what that meant for our future. I later found out that, according to my aunt, my parents were never married. Was my mother relieved or afraid or sad? Or all of those things?

After our father left, the bills mounted and the house became too much for our mother to afford, so we moved into a much smaller place. For two years, from 1963 to 1965, we lived in a house on 44th Street that was a cramped duplex with a small room in the back for me. When Paul Howard visited home from the Air Force, he had to sleep in the dining room.

Our mother became ill shortly after we moved. Kendall told me he heard our mother screaming in pain many times. Our sister, Kathy, had a friend, Judy, whose mother was a nurse. She would come over often to check on our mother and rub the tenderness out of her leg or check the sores on her face that seemed to worsen with each day.

Our mother was soon hospitalized and, while her spirits generally remained high, she had good days and bad days. The doctor diagnosed her with leukemia and said that she had only a few weeks to live. She succumbed to the illness just two weeks short of my twenty-second birthday.

The government sent a special nurse to my house to help take care of me while our mother was in the hospital, but after our mother died, my siblings took over and started taking care of me. Kendall helped as much as he could and then left for the service in Vietnam. Val, Laurie, and Steven (then age ten) were left to care for me.

My father made only brief appearances a few times a year, coming in from Dallas, and sent Western Union telegrams from time to time. He showed up for a while when my mother became sick, and he stayed for the funeral. He helped us move into another home on 17th Street, but then he was back on the road. We were on our own. The Shriners were kind enough to help with visits from time to time, and churches checked to make sure we had things we needed, but without my siblings' constant care, such as daily turning, bathing, and bedsore care, I was helpless.

I know I should have been sad when my mother died, but it was mostly a numb feeling. I felt a vast emptiness, like having someone there and then not. It is hard for hearing people to understand, but when you are deaf and you have no communication with someone, it is hard to get close to that person. That is what it was like for me, with my mother. I missed her and felt the fact that she was gone, and I am truly grateful for all she did for me, but I never really knew her.

Val helped as much as she could until she became pregnant and had to move away, and Kathy had gotten married right after high school. So it was just Laurie and Steven until Paul Howard came back from the service. Our father and other adults came and went, but Laurie and Steven both had to take care of me in the mornings before they went to school. Laurie made breakfast, and they both would change my catheter and empty my urinary bag, and then Steven would slip out into the darkness to run his paper route before walking two miles to Gatewood elementary school every morning. I imagine what Steven or Laurie must have thought when they heard the other kids at school complain about their lives. This was an ordinary day for them, and I never saw them complain about anything.

I spent my days mostly reading everything I could get my hands on. I craved information of any kind. I loved nature and animals and wanted to learn anything I could about them. I would prop my books up against the special table and painstakingly turn the pages with my paralyzed fists. I would pull my thumb out either with the other fist or with my mouth just enough to push the page over, or I would shove the page over with my entire fist and hope I didn't push too many pages at once. It was frustrating at times, but I managed. I had ample time to perfect my technique.

I was fascinated by the subject of the possibility of life on other planets, UFOs, and outer space. I asked for books on these subjects and read as much as I could. So much of this puzzled me as much as it intrigued me. The more I read, the more questions I had. Is there life out there?

I had a big window with a great view, and I would spend a lot of time trying to imagine what it was like out among the stars and planets. The day my brothers and sisters brought me a telescope, I thought I would burst with excitement. I had something to fill the lonely nights. Staring at the stars and planets for hours became a wonderful pastime for me, and I treasured it. I would study my astronomy books and share what I had learned with Steven, who, of all of my siblings, was the most eager to be my star-gazing pupil.

I also watched nature shows on TV. Those were some of my favorites. I was particularly interested in birds and bees and their habits. Even though I could not hear the narrator on the television, I could see the beauty of nature and watch the animals and their movements. To me, it was incredible.

One day, my brothers surprised me with something they had ordered in the mail for me: a bee-keeping kit. They placed the transparent, two-sided unit into the window where I could see it clearly. Clear plastic tubing led from the unit to the outside and provided entrance and exit to a hive for the honeybees. It was amazing for me to observe. I read all the accompanying literature on honeybees and their habits, and I really enjoyed sharing what I learned with Steven when he came into my room.

One time, I very seriously told him that I learned the bees would break through the glass and sting him at night. He gave me a horrified look, which I returned with a huge grin, and he knew I was just kidding and was so relieved and laughed.

These were special times for Steven and me. I think he really looked forward to our moments together because our parents were not there for him and he needed some encouragement from someone older. Even though I was stuck in the bed, I felt a sense of purpose. I could teach him things. I taught him to fingerspell and communicate with me. I taught him things about nature and things I had read. Most of all, he learned about life. He learned responsibility, and he learned about hope and about not giving up in the face of adversity. He learned about love and about the important things that you should not take for granted—mostly family. He saw that I became frustrated sometimes but that I never gave up hope and that I tried to stay as positive as possible and keep my sense of humor. He saw that I was on his side and mostly that I loved him and was there for him, no matter what.

I also spent many of those long days reading books on how to play chess. I wanted to master the game. I asked my siblings to bring me anything they could find about this subject. I studied diligently and asked for a chessboard so I could practice how to move the pieces. This was a marvelous way to occupy my time, of which I had a lot. When I figured out how each of the pieces moved, I needed an opponent. Steven was more than willing to spend many afternoons as my student, learning the game and playing chess with me for hours. Our bond grew even stronger. He had such patience for such a young boy.

During those years I was at home, it was interesting to note the ways in which different people reacted to me and my condition. Some acted natural and treated me like any other sick friend. They were pleasant and supportive. But many others gave me the impression that they thought me useless and that my life was a waste. Some seemed to indicate that an insufficient faith in God was the reason I couldn't walk. Some thought that I should repent of my sins and be "healed" before it was too late.

Sometimes I felt victimized by these types of people. True, I did not come from what would be considered a "religious" family. I did not consider myself as being religious, and I had no church home or personal minister. Still, I knew that despite deafness and paralysis, I was human. I also knew that I believed in God and sometimes I felt alone and confused. Was I doing the right things in my own eyes but the wrong things in God's eyes? What bad had I actually done, and what should I be doing? Was I simply the victim of cruel fate, or was I being punished? Should I feel guilt? Did I feel loved? Time and again, it seemed, I was being asked to ponder such questions. I knew that I had to search for the answers as to what was right for me and hold fast to any source of hope and courage.

Many preachers of many denominations visited me. Someone would eventually tell a preacher about me, and so he would come. I know these preachers meant well, but I frankly found them to be of little help—confusing, really.

I remember the first preacher who came to see me. He was tall, looked about fifty years old, and was difficult to understand. He knew no sign language. I could read some things from his lips, but mostly I had to ask him to write down what he had to say. I tried to be patient with him, but it became quite tedious. He asked me if I read the Bible.

"Oh, yes," I said.

"Where is your Bible?"

I indicated a shelf against the wall, and he ambled over to the shelf. To my chagrin, the Bible was covered with a layer of dust. Well, I hadn't said that I read it daily. Still, I felt that he was accusing me of lying when he quietly laid the Bible on my bedside table, suggested that I read it, and left.

When I read the Bible at the Convalescent Center, it had not made much sense, and I had abandoned it. Now I decided to give it another try. I reached over and carefully cracked it open. I gazed at the pages as the unfamiliar words and perplexing passages sprang at me. I had heard that Jesus was a friend but had never learned much more than that. Now it seemed that I could not understand what all I was reading meant. I slammed the book shut in frustration and put it back on the table.

A short time later, I received a visit from a preacher from another church.

He asked me, through writing notes, if I believed in God, and I said, "Yes."

I told him about the first preacher's visit.

"Oh," he promptly informed me, "that preacher and his church are no good."

He proceeded to tell me that their beliefs were not right and that only his church subscribed to the correct doctrine. Now I was even more confused—how was I to know which churches were right and which weren't?

As preachers from many different denominations came and went, I seemed to hear the same conflict repeated over and over. Naturally, each preacher wanted me to join his particular church. But how was I to choose? At length, after a Lutheran minister visited me several times, I joined his church. But now I do not believe it was an act of strong conviction, and I did not attend the church.

I came to the conclusion that if the different churches claimed to base their respective doctrines on the Bible and, yet, could not agree on a common doctrine, then it was up to me to try to find out for myself just what the Bible's teachings were. I began reading the Bible more and comparing what I read with what I had been told. If I happened upon a passage that I didn't understand, I would ask the preachers. If their explanations conflicted, I would simply decide for myself what I thought the meaning was.

I became quite interested in the Bible and longed to find out more from it. I resolved never to give up studying the Bible. I felt that the scriptures were becoming very clear to me. I felt that God had wonderful plans for everyone, including even me. I felt hope.

Many years later, after I settled in Tulsa, Oklahoma, I met a deaf preacher named George Peknik. I joined his Baptist church and was happy there for many years. His church insisted on baptism by immersion, and, though I do not think they had done many quadriplegics before, there could be no exception. So there I went, colostomy appliances and all, to the baptismal font. The Lord must have smiled in amusement that day because it was a very clumsy and awkward affair. I'm sure it would have made an interesting video.

One afternoon, in the spring of 1967, I got another interesting visit. This time, it was not a preacher. A man from the Vocational Rehabilitation (VR) program in Oklahoma City came and asked me if I wanted to go to a VR facility in Hot Springs, Arkansas. I told him, yes, I would very much like to go. At first, my father did not think it was a good idea and did not want me to go. But I saw it as perhaps an opportunity for more self-improvement and independence, and so my wishes prevailed. The VR people gave me a test, an evaluation, in my home before I left for Hot Springs.

My father and my brother Kendall, then seventeen, drove me in our old DeSoto to Hot Springs. My father let Kendall drive until he sideswiped the steel suspension bridge as we crossed the Ouachita River. When we arrived at the training facility, Kendall opened the door and the weight of my body launched me out of the car almost onto the pavement. Kendall had to catch me and couldn't help letting out a nervous laugh. It made me mad. He apologized, though.

The VR facility paid for the training and living expenses for me, and I was very excited and glad to be out of the house for a change. However, whatever was to have been accomplished at the facility did not work out. It turned into an unhappy experience. Every day, I still had the miserable problem of sweating and chills when I was in my wheelchair. No one there could help me with this problem. They, like the doctors before them, thought that I must be worried, fearful, or homesick, which I denied. The counselors became concerned. I also had a lot of problems with the colostomy appliances while I was there.

As a result, after I was there for four weeks, I felt that I could bear it no longer and asked to go back home. I was very disappointed. Two days after I came home, I had a terrible nightmare. I was inside a huge piece of foam that had many holes of varying sizes, and there was no gravity. I fought, seemingly for hours, trying to get out of that awful foam.

When I awoke, I found myself in a strange world with strange people all around my bed. I looked at the man standing near the bed and didn't know who he was, but when I tried thinking very hard and my mind cleared, I knew that he was my father. A woman stood next to him, and it took me a while to realize that she was my sister. There were two other men in the room I did not know, and when I asked my sister about them, she said that they were paramedics.

She told me that I was screaming, fighting, and carrying on for a long time, and when they could not wake me up, they knew something was wrong. She said I had bitten my father's hand and my own tongue. Sure enough, I noticed then that my tongue was cut. So what had brought all this on? I think I had some sort of inner conflict resulting from the Hot Springs experience, perhaps even a fear of being taken back. At any rate, we were able to send away the paramedics, and I silently thanked God that everything was okay. I was home again and wondering where my life would take me next.

# 7

## New Home, New Challenges

In fall 1969, I was reading a newspaper called the *OKIE*, a publication about deaf people in Oklahoma. There was a small news item about a deaf quadriplegic, named James Harrell, who lived at Ranch Terrace Nursing Home in Sapulpa, Oklahoma. After reading the article, I began to speculate about what life in the nursing home would be like. I wondered if there might be several young disabled people living there, and I envisioned companionship, along with sharing common interests and common problems.

I decided to write James Harrell a letter. He wrote back, asking me to come live with them, like a family. I thought I couldn't after I discovered it would cost $500 a month to live there, but then I found that welfare would pay the cost, and I immediately decided to move. The nursing home sent an ambulance to my home to move me to Sapulpa. It was in February 1970. I had just turned twenty-eight.

James was somewhat older. I would guess about thirty-five. He was a painter who created beautiful paintings with a paintbrush he held in his teeth. There was also another "quad" who lived at the home at that time, named Jim St. Pierre. Jim was the youngest of the three of us; he was probably twenty-four. Jim was not deaf, but he had learned ways to communicate with James and me.

When I moved there, I thought I would room with James, but that was not the case. Two people were assigned to each room. James had tons of stuff in his room, and he had an old man for a roommate. Jim also had a lot of things, and he too roomed with an old man. Old men have very few things. I was assigned a room

45

next door to James' room, and I shared this room with a man who was senile and very old. I quickly realized that this was not a place for the young and disabled, but rather for the elderly and sick. We three quads constituted our own little minority.

I had a regular hospital-type bed, just like I had at home, and my regular push wheelchair. I started trying to use the wheelchair again and found that, as always, I was still plagued with sweating and chills whenever I sat in the thing. James was immediately aware of my problem and suggested that I try placing a piece of plywood, with the center cut out, across the seat of the wheelchair. We found someone to cut a piece of plywood the size of the seat and then cut a large U out of the center. The idea seemed crazy, but after so many years of frustration, I was ready to try anything. It looked less comfortable than before, but to my surprise it worked. Somehow it relieved the pressure on my hip bones, and I had no more sweating and chills from then on.

Such a simple thing. I felt that nine years of my life had been partially wasted because I had not had the benefit of such a simple thing, which James had learned about at the Rusk Rehabilitation Center in New York.

Our (the "quads") main concern was finding ways to keep ourselves busy from day to day. We were always bored, so we tried to think up things to do to pass the time. Those ranged from activities that might be considered somewhat educational, like strolling outside and trying to identify the different kinds of birds, to the really inane, like strolling around the parking lot trying to figure out which car belonged to which nurse. The nursing home had books about birds, and James already knew a lot of the birds' names. But it does not take long to identify all the birds common to eastern Oklahoma or to tire of trying to identify the nurses' cars in the parking lot.

We tried flying kites when the weather was right. One might ask how a quadriplegic can get a kite in the air. You eventually learn to adapt whatever movement, strength, and dexterity you have to the task at hand, and you will find that, surprisingly, you can do more things than you might think. Of course, we were not exactly racing in the wind across an open field. But the tug of the string as the kite caught the breeze was a good feeling, and it was fun to watch the kites in motion. Sometimes the nurses lined up inside at the windows to watch. Most of the time we never got the kites back—they wound up stuck in some tree. Soon the kites joined the birds and the nurses' cars; they lost our interest.

"There must be something else we can do," I said to James one day.

Really, I said this to him every other day. We thought about it. I did not read very much now. Having companions around diverted my attention from books, and I guess I had become tired of reading. Finally, I came up with something I thought had possibilities.

"Why don't we buy a horse trailer and convert it into a way to get around, wheelchairs and all," I asked.

A horse trailer would have a ramp for loading and unloading, I explained.

James didn't think I was serious at first, but when he saw otherwise, he said, "Well, why not check it out?"

So we collected information and cost figures on horse trailers, the installation of springs and shock absorbers, the addition of windows on the sides, and other things, and came up with a total cost of possibly a thousand dollars. Not too bad, we guessed, although we had no clear idea as to where the money would come from and who we would get to pull it around—friends or anyone who came to visit, maybe? We told one of the nurses about the idea, and she thought it sounded interesting. She said that she would try to help us find a trailer. I also told my family about it, but they never did anything to help. I think they thought the idea was crazy. As time went on, I began to realize that we would not get the trailer, and the idea soon faded.

Around the same time, I heard about a nursing home in Dallas, Texas, with a special program for deaf patients. I was intrigued, so I wrote a letter to Fairhaven Nursing Home asking about their facility. I received a response explaining their services and saying that they, indeed, had many deaf patients there. I became anxious to go, but James did not want to go because he had two brothers in Tulsa, only a few miles from Sapulpa. I decided to investigate a possible transfer to Fairhaven anyway. I asked the Oklahoma Welfare Department if they could help me with my expenses, but they refused. When I asked for help from the Texas Welfare Department, they informed me that they could not help me until I had been a resident of Texas for one year. I was disappointed and decided to give up on moving to another nursing home.

I became increasingly restless with my life at Ranch Terrace and more impatient with conditions there. I did not think the home was properly equipped to handle people like me. Perhaps I expected too much of them, but there seemed to be continual problems with the nursing and attending staff. Nurses came and went on three different shifts. Some were pleasant enough, but others were not.

I remember one nurse in particular whom I found most exasperating. She seemed to pay very little attention to me or my special needs. Many of the nurses did not seem to have much patience with me. I could see that the problem stemmed from a combination of two reasons: poor communication between us and the nature and stress of their duties. When you are deaf and must rely on someone else for help with just about everything, communication is both critical and difficult. The nursing staff did not know sign language, except for obvious hand gestures and a few simple and frequently used signs that I taught them. Most communication had to be done with notes. But who had time to wait for a guy with a pen or pencil clenched between his teeth to write out a complete and comprehensive note? They were usually too busy. My efforts to write a note often failed because the nurse brusquely interrupted me or simply left the room.

Sometimes I felt that I was merely the object on which they took out their irritation, and it was often useless to expect an explanation. One afternoon, one of the aides grabbed my wheelchair in the hallway and forced me to go to bed at that instant, even though it was early afternoon and I was in the middle of a conversation with Jim. I asked for a few more minutes, but she ignored me and pushed me all the way into bed.

I asked her again, "Why?" All she said was, "Shut up!"

At times, I thought some of them were inclined to be unnecessarily rough. Sometimes I could see that it was necessary to manhandle a patient in the interests of all concerned, but I often thought that I was—and others were—shaken or roughly thrown around merely in the interest of the nurse's disposition.

Other times, it was difficult to know how much to insist upon and how much to overlook. There was the case of the bedsore that could have been prevented if one of the nurse's aides had done her job properly. For some reason my bowels had soiled my bedding (and my bottom), and I called in the aide to clean it up. I could see that she only partially did the job.

Throughout the years, I had had my share of discomfort from bedsores, and I had learned the importance of cleanliness in attempting to prevent them. I asked her to clean up the rest, but she refused and left the room. I was aware and afraid of what would happen, but I was given no chance to explain or complain, and I let the matter go.

The nurse's aide for the next shift became upset when she saw what had happened, and she said, "Now you will have a sore."

Sure enough, I was uncomfortable for two months while waiting for the sore to heal.

Sometimes the nurses were not so much careless as merely thoughtless. For instance, I did a certain amount of painting for entertainment. The nurses would bring me the paint in some jars, place the jars on the table, and leave before opening them, forgetting that I couldn't open them myself. I would have no choice but to call them back. I would give a loud toot on the whistle that I kept at my bedside. I could not call out "Nurse!" as the hearing patients did to attract the attention of a passing nurse, so I often used my whistle. Of course, they were already cross when they reentered my room because they had been called back so soon.

With hand on hip and scowl on face, they would say, "What do you want?"

Occasionally residents resorted to bribery in order to get help or get things done. Every now and then, I saw it happen. One time, in order to persuade a nurse to help him get out of bed, James had to promise her a necklace. I do not know the value of the necklace, but James kept a stock of things like that on hand. Whenever nurses refused to do something for him, he would just get out one of his little trinkets.

I tried to understand the nurses' position. I could see the kind of things they had to deal with and the kind of days they had to put in. There were about five nurses on duty at all times to care for approximately one hundred patients. I could see that they were often harried and overworked. They were often behind in their duties and had time to do only what had to be done in order to catch up.

I saw the constant and unpleasant interruptions that they had to contend with every day. One night, my roommate, who was half out of his mind and strapped in his bed because he was prone to leave the building and wander off the grounds at night, began to play with and eat the excrement he had deposited in his bed. When I saw this, I gave out a toot on my trusty whistle for the nurse. She stuck him in the shower, changed the bedding, strapped him back in bed, and, just in the nick of time before she left, stopped him from drinking from a cup in which he had deposited his urine. I also saw an old woman running down the hallway, her legs spread wide apart and the hems of her skirt lifted high, dropping excrement every step of the way. Although there was a bathroom in each bedroom, she was obviously confused and did not know where to go. I saw the nurses' hectic days, and I tried to understand. I tried to be nice to them and to justify their reactions when they seemed intemperate or inconsiderate. But sometimes it was hard, and things didn't seem fair.

Sometimes I would go to the office and try to explain my complaints. More often than not, it didn't work, either because the nurses supported each other or because they did not clearly understand my complaints. I knew I would just have to be strong, grit my teeth, and accept it all quietly or it would be even harder to deal with in the long run. However, even though I had resolved to accept it, I could be difficult and lash out. One time when I felt particularly frustrated, I deliberately knocked over the pitcher of water on the table by my bed. Water spilled everywhere.

The nurse came, I started to do it again, and she said, "Don't you dare!"

I thought that was rather funny. Actually, I guess it was sad.

James, Jim, and I always talked about what else we could do to liven up our lives at what we had come to call "the prison." Perhaps the most absorbing and constructive project we came up with was the vegetable garden. The area next to the home was vacant, neglected, and polluted, with a lot of ugly trees, thorn bushes, and weeds growing wild. One summer, the owner of the nursing home made arrangements with the landowners—the school district, as I understood, since it later built a school building on part of the land—to clean up the lot. The school board hired some boys to clean up the grounds, and some men came and cut down some of the trees.

We scattered some seeds and watched them for a few weeks, but the maintenance people didn't have time to care for the garden full time. The plants started drying up and dying, and I started worrying. Then Jim had a suggestion. The nursing home had five large air conditioners on top of the roof, and his idea was to catch the dripping water from the air conditioners in some empty twenty-gallon garbage cans.

I put two or three cans under the roof where the water dripped. It took only one day to fill the large cans, which gave us plenty of water. I would dip a bucket into the can, carry it all the way over to the garden, and water the plants. I went back and forth, back and forth. I did most of the watering and hoeing by myself. I used tools with extra-long handles to do the gardening. Some of my family helped us, but only when they came on the occasional weekend. The garden looked beautiful, with lush, green leaves. A few months later, there were fully ripe tomatoes, hot peppers, onions, watermelons, and cucumbers.

All of us enjoyed watching the garden grow, and we were proud of it. Our garden had dirt paths between the rows of vegetables so we could guide our wheelchairs through in order to reach the plants for watering, weeding, and picking the vegetables. By now all three of us had electric wheelchairs. One morning, Jim wanted to take a close look at the garden. Somehow, he got stuck in the soft dirt. I tried to get him out, but I got stuck also. Then James tried and got stuck, too.

I said, "We must get out of this ourselves; do our best."

We tried very hard to push with our bodies, back and forth, in our wheelchairs until somehow Jim was able to push James out, but Jim was still stuck. James came around behind me and pushed me out, and I tied a rope to Jim's chair and pulled him out. All of this took so long that it was almost time for lunch. We were lucky we solved our dilemma ourselves because the home would not have let us have a garden if they knew we had any problems.

That was not the only time I got stuck in the dirt outside, however. James and I had been talking about sneaking out of the building and going deep through the trees for a change. One day we did. We were looking for unusual birds or anything interesting and new.

I was the first to sneak out. I went through the woods and weeds, over soil that was very soft and marshy, and got stuck. James came to help me out of my predicament. He tied a rope to the back bumper of his wheelchair and to the upper back of my wheelchair and then started to pull me. My chair tilted way back, and my legs went high in the air. I felt like I was riding a wild horse. It is a wonder that we did not tip the chair over, but we were lucky. James finally pulled me out, laughing at the way we had done it.

A crab apple tree sat on the vacant land next to the nursing home property. It was February, but it was very warm and sunny and Jim, James, and I noticed that nests of worms were developing on the tree. We became concerned and decided that our next project would be to do something about the crab apple tree. Jim thought we could set the nests on fire with gasoline or perhaps spray them with pesticide. He tried to recruit someone to help us but had no luck.

About two months later—during which the nests continued to spread—a friend of mine named Roy came for a visit. He was interested in our garden, and when I told him about our concern for the crab apple tree, he said he would be glad to help us destroy the worms. He said he would return in about three weeks and would try to do something about it then, but he did not come. The nests opened and thousands of worms crawled everywhere and ate most of the leaves off the tree.

One of the aides said her husband would come and spray the tree with pesticide. The next morning, James was very excited and told me to come outside with him.

"Look at that," he said.

Thousands of worms were writhing and dying on the ground under the tree. About that time, Roy showed up, saying that he had come to destroy the worm nests. We pointed out that he had arrived too late, but then we noticed that there were still many live worms up in the tree. So we decided to do something about it. We found a long wooden pole. Roy tied rags onto the end of the pole and set them aflame with gasoline. He set the tree on fire without a problem and succeeded in destroying the nests high in the tree. When the fire went out, he put the pole down on the grass to pour on more gasoline, but the rags were still hot and flames sprang up and ignited his shirt. Roy thought fast, rolled on the ground, and quickly took off his shirt. He was rushed to the nearest hospital with bad burns on his right arm and part of his shoulder. He stayed in the hospital for three weeks. I'm sure it must have been expensive. Fortunately, insurance was able to cover his bills.

I was very upset about what had happened to Roy, and I felt useless because I was not able to help him. I was glad that he wasn't injured too badly. His brother tried to sue the nursing home, which surprised me because I didn't feel it had been the nursing home's fault. Roy's brother eventually lost the suit because the tree was outside the boundaries of the nursing home property. A short time later, because of all this, we got a note from the owner of the nursing home saying that there would be no more gardening.

I told her that nothing like that would happen again, but she said, "Absolutely no garden!"

I begged her to allow me to at least do some gardening in some plastic buckets. She said she would think about it and let me know what she decided. About a week later, she said okay. She didn't tell me how many buckets I could have, and I don't think she was very happy when I got twenty to twenty-five from a nearby farmer. But I didn't care. By this time, the school district had built a building and was using more of its land, so further gardening on the previously vacant lot would not have been feasible and likely not allowed.

Sometimes, for fun, James would chase a squirrel all over the area in his wheelchair until it ran away. Once, when he was sure the squirrel had buried some pecans in the ground, he searched the area where he had seen the squirrel digging, but he couldn't find any. Smart squirrel! We gave some of the pecans that we were able to gather to a girl who cooked at the home, and she put them in some fudge for us.

These things gave us something to do, and we had a lot of fun, too.

We also had an ongoing preoccupation with an old man at the home named Bob. He was about 70 years old. I suppose he was only old and cranky, but he seemed to have some kind of resentment toward James and me. He was always giving us a hard time and making fun of us because we used sign language. Once he tried to ruin the TDD we used to communicate on the phone, and he would move a chair to block us from reaching it.

There was also an old deaf man who mowed the grass and cleaned up the yard at the nursing home. James and I would spend some time outside talking with him. One day he found some bottles of beer and whiskey in the hedge. He put the bottles on the windowsill outside and went inside to call for the R.N. By the time she got there, however, the bottles were gone.

On other occasions, beer, whiskey, and cigarettes were found in different places outside. We decided to try and figure out who was hiding these things. We suspected it might be Old Man Bob, and we knew he was not allowed to drink alcoholic beverages or smoke cigarettes because they were bad for his health and conflicted with the prescribed medication he was taking at the time.

I started watching him at every opportunity when he was outside, with the binoculars I used for bird-watching. One day I saw him drinking some whiskey deep in the wooded area behind the home. Another day, James found some more bottles hidden in some bushes. When Old Man Bob learned that James had found his cache, he got angry and messed up one of James' oil paintings with a cigarette butt.

On another occasion, I found several bottles of beer under some old logs and other trash. I thought to myself, "This is better than an Easter-egg hunt!"

Old Man Bob continued to hide more beer and whiskey in new hiding places outside, and I kept finding them and carrying the beer to my room. He would get angry and try to be more careful to find better hiding places, but I would still spot him through the window each time.

One time, my father came for a visit. I asked him if he wanted some beer, and he said sure. I showed him a bottle of Coors hidden under the grass next to a telephone pole. He was surprised. He acted like I must have planted some kind of magic seed and waited for beer to grow. We put the bottle in a small red icebox, which I put in my room for a while to cool down. Later, Old Man Bob came and asked my dad how he had liked the beer. He played innocent, but the next day, I noticed my long aluminum pole with the hook on the tip was broken. It was what I had used to pry about the logs and weeds, looking for his bottles of beer.

We had a lot of fun with that old man, but I began to feel bad about it. I had taken about thirteen bottles of his beer, and I knew it had cost him a lot. So I decided to buy a six-pack of Coors to give to him at Christmas, but somehow I never remembered to do it. Such were our diversions at the nursing home.

Paul Howard, Kendall, Laurie, and Steven came to visit. Laurie and Steven decided it would be nice to get me out in the fresh air for a walk, away from the smell and confines of the nursing home. I loved getting outside and was excited to go. We had fun. It was always so good to see family and forget about the boredom of my everyday life. We strolled around the countryside, my siblings taking turns pushing my wheelchair and turning me around in silly circles and laughing. I was so glad to breathe the fresh air and to be with my family and away from the stresses of the nursing home. I almost forgot for a little while about everything. I felt young again and free.

Suddenly, the weight of my chair shifted and I lost control. My chair rocked sideways and, before I knew it, crashed to the ground. Laurie rushed to lift my wheelchair upright and, with Steven's help, managed to get me back in my chair again. I made them promise not to say a word for fear I would not be allowed this freedom to leave the grounds again. They agreed.

I did not tell them that if I had broken a bone, it could be serious enough to cause a life-threatening infection. I did not want to worry them. Worst of all, to me, my freedom was worth the silence. I would take my chances.

Paul Howard, Kendall, our father, and I went fishing one time at Lake Hefner. I was having a hard time getting my fishing line out far enough, and we were trying to come up with some way for me, with my limited arm movement, to cast the line and keep it out far enough. My brilliant idea was to use a helium balloon to keep the line afloat. We brought the helium balloon on top of the old Pontiac. It was about four feet in diameter, beige in color, and we attached it to the fishing rod. We deemed it a complete failure when we had to cut the line and watch the balloon float away, but we couldn't help laughing as we watched it go. I treasured these times with my brothers.

In the nursing home, I always felt as if I was in prison, and there were times I felt as if I was being treated like nothing more than a vegetable. Old men came and went in my room. One would die, the next would come in, then he, too, would die, and still another would take his place—on and on, until I started wondering if I was next.

One day, a bright spot in the form of a ten-year-old girl appeared in my room. She was freckle faced, curly haired, and curious, but something about her was different. She approached me in my bed, where I so often spent my days, but did not speak.

In her face, I saw a question.

"Why are you here," she silently asked.

I knew she was puzzled about why I did not look old or sick like the others. I moved my lips and gestured the best I could to explain that I had broken my neck. To my surprise, she understood.

The little girl, with the few signs she knew and mostly with her broken speech, told me that she, herself, was deaf. She had just moved to a new school nearby and was the only deaf student in a non-signing "oral" program. Her parents had told her about James and me and encouraged her to meet us while she visited her grandmother at the nursing home. The girl's name was Glenna. I began to look forward to her visits. I would teach her signs, and she would borrow my books or other items. She would ask me questions about life, ideas, people, anything. I could see that she was as lonely as I was. Our friendship lasted for five years, until her grandmother passed away. Glenna grew into an intelligent, fascinating, fifteen-year-old. When she left, I missed her visits greatly and wished her well. I knew she would make a difference in the world. I had no idea then how much she would accomplish.*

---

* Glenna Cooper grew up to become an American Sign Language instructor, a leader in the Deaf community, and an advocate for Deaf rights.

Then came Randy, a deaf boy who had a car accident in which he struck a tree and badly damaged part of his brain. About three years after his accident, he moved in with me as my roommate. But his talk in sign language was very strange to me, and crazy. Sometimes he thought he was in heaven and that we were all angels. He sometimes got angry because he thought we all had wings except him.

I think he used drugs and that was what confused his thoughts. His body moved shakily, and it was very difficult for him to feed himself. The nurses and aides could not communicate with him at all. Sometimes he was violent as he tried to force his way outside, as though he, too, felt himself in prison. It was difficult to calm him down and to reason with him.

There seemed to be nothing I could do to help poor Randy. He always seemed to be in trouble. The owner of the home wanted him to stay and tried to reason with him, but eventually she had to ask him to leave. I felt sorry for him. I don't know what happened to him. I only hope he was able to find a good place to live.

As for myself, I tried to cooperate and to cause as few problems as possible. Still, in the nine years I spent there, I never felt at home. But I did not think going back home to my father's house would be a good decision to make. In the first place, I did not feel it would be fair to my family to cast the responsibility for my day-to-day care back upon them. After all these years, living at home would not have been the same as before, and it would have been an infringement on all our freedoms, mine as well as theirs. It would have been a step backward, toward dependence, when what I really wanted was more independence. I kept feeling that a more independent life was possible for me.

One of the aides at the nursing home was a very pretty and sweet girl, and when she looked at me and smiled, it made me feel good. I was attracted to her. After she gave me a bath one day, as she put my T-shirt on me, I quickly pulled her neck down toward me and kissed her on the lips. We both felt high for a moment. But when the other aides heard about it, they made fun of her, and that drove her away. I understood because I felt useless, and I didn't like that feeling.

Love is important to everyone—even quads. It always felt good just to get a kiss and a hug from an aide in exchange for a birthday present from me. I kept thinking how I would like to find a nice disabled woman who would need me as I needed her. We would help each other and live in a mobile home or apartment. That would be a joy for me and for her, too, I would hope. It's the person inside that counts.

One time, I was telling a nurse my thoughts—how I longed to be independent, have a girlfriend, have a good job.

She looked at me incredulously and said, "You? You are ugly! Who would want you?"

Another nurse heard her and told her not to say things like that.

I knew that the nurses often talked bad about me, but I realized that it was their problem and not mine. Sometimes, though, I thought about the possibilities of really becoming independent and of finding a girl who would love me. I realized that it would be something rare and special if it did happen.

It was then that I realized my three dreams in life: to be independent, to get a job, and to get married. I knew I would achieve these three goals someday. I did not know how, but I knew in my heart that I would.

About two years before I left the nursing home, I grew my beard. It would stay with me always. One might think I grew it out of convenience to avoid having to shave, but shaving was not all that difficult for me. One of the nurses suggested that I ought to grow a beard because she thought I would look good in one, so I tried it. I liked it, and I kept it.

# 8

## Independence

Finally, opportunity came to call. I didn't know it, but my life was about to change. Judy Peknik, George's wife, often came to visit James and me. One day, she asked me if I would like to have a job.

I emphatically said, "Yes!"

Gerald Davis, a counselor from the Oklahoma Vocational Rehabilitation Department, came to see me. Gerald said that Judy had told him about me. In sign language, he asked me what my hopes and goals were. About a year passed, during which Gerald came to see me often and we talked about job possibilities.

I became more impatient to work and to be on my own. But first, I would have to go to the Tulsa Rehabilitation Center at Hillcrest Hospital to be evaluated. Once I passed that evaluation, I would go to Wilson Rehabilitation Center in Fishersville, Virginia, for training.

Gerald Davis was the kind of person who really believed in the Vocational Rehabilitation mission. He believed in anyone's potential to become successful. He was a true advocate for people with disabilities. This was a time when services were not provided for people who lived in nursing homes. How do you live independently if you do not have a job? The nursing home had control of my small government social security allotment. In order to serve me, Gerald had to go to his supervisor and ask that the rules be changed.

This was also a time when counselors could not send a person out of state for job training—yet another obstacle Gerald had to overcome. He had to ask Oklahoma VR to send a deaf "quad" to

The local newspaper did a story on Don. Bernadette Pruitt, "After a Decade, Message Heard: 'I'm Lonely and Thirst for Freedom'," *Tulsa World*, 1979. Photos by Mel Root.

Virginia, to one of only a few programs in the country that could provide deaf/quad vocational services. But this was not new for Gerald Davis. He had a history of taking on difficult cases, such as the case of an athlete from Oklahoma State University who had broken his neck and become a quadriplegic. Gerald sent this man, flat on his back on a hospital bed and hooked to IVs, to college classes every day.

Gerald believed anyone could work, given the opportunity, and he stubbornly did not give up. I was the type of person Gerald did not have to push in order to succeed. He just had to remove the obstacles in my path. I just knew I could do it, and so did he.

It was 1979, and I was now thirty-seven years old. From April 2 through July 22, I stayed at the Tulsa Rehabilitation Center and participated in their program of evaluation and therapy. There were tests of manual dexterity; they wanted to see what kinds of things I could do with my arms and hands. For instance, they gave me nuts and bolts to see how well I could put them together. There were math tests, speech therapy sessions, sexual counseling sessions, and psychological evaluations. There was training in personal care and hygiene and in independent living functions, such as cooking. There was physical therapy and exercise twice a day, five days a week. There were also some fun times and recreational activities, such as craft projects, movies and dances, field trips and picnics. Twice, I was allowed to go out on my own—once using the Tulsa bus transit system—to shopping centers to shop for clothes and to have my eyeglasses repaired. Everything went well, and I was pleased with myself for the accomplishment.

I was grateful for the experiences at the center, but I also had a certain amount of bad luck during those three and a half months. One day, the therapist tried to put me on the mat by herself. She had never done this before, but she couldn't find anyone else to help her. When she tugged sharply to lift my waist and hips, something suddenly snapped, and it hurt very much. She looked worried and wanted me to go see the doctor. I didn't think too much of it, but a few minutes later, I started to get very chilled and started sweating. They took me to the x-ray room.

The next morning, the doctor came in and said, in simple signs, "It is broken."

I had sustained an intertrochanteric (to quote the record) fracture in my left hip. I felt so disappointed because I was afraid I would never feel comfortable in the wheelchair again. The doctor recommended against doing any surgical procedure at the time, because he felt a non-union of the fracture might be more acceptable in the long run than the stiffness that might occur as a result of surgery.

I suffered severe sweating for about eight weeks, but the hip healed well with no problems. I was relieved and happy because my therapy program had not really been interrupted by the fracture. Then the center lost a lot of my clothes, even though my name was marked on them. Someone lost five pairs of pants, two T-shirts, one shirt, and three pairs of socks. The center couldn't compensate me because insurance wouldn't pay for the loss of clothes, so I had to buy my own replacements. That was an expensive loss for me.

Once again, I had problems with aides and attendants. One night, when I was in the shower and an aide was helping me bathe, I asked her for some shampoo for my beard so that I could wash it myself. She refused because she was behind schedule and in a hurry. I called for the R.N. and told her that I wanted some shampoo. The aide told her she had already washed my beard with shampoo. She lied, of course, and the R.N. believed her and scolded me. I understood that I must hold my peace because it wouldn't do any good to try to convince her.

One night, one of the aides brought my supper tray with a steak, a baked potato, and vegetables. She helped me cut the steak, and then she picked up a piece of the steak and ate it. I didn't really mind that, but when she found it too tough and had trouble chewing it, she spit it out into the middle of my plate. She stood there looking at me as if I were nothing but a dumb vegetable. She didn't worry about me making a complaint to the R.N. because she knew they wouldn't believe me, because the whole thing was so unbelievable. I knew it would do no good to become angry because they would just say that I was acting childish and write it down in my chart. That would make me look bad. Plus, by the time I managed to get paper and struggled to get a pen in my mouth to write, who would be patient enough to see what I had to say?

As usual, I tried to understand and rationalize their behavior, but conflicts like these slowly began to defeat my spirit. It seemed that everywhere I lived, it was the same. I could only try to keep peace within myself and wait for the time when, maybe, I could be truly independent—if that was ever possible or just a dream.

During my stay at the center, I had another strange dream. I dreamed that I saw a tree with no leaves. I remember it never moved, never changed. It fascinated me. I never tired of looking at it. It seemed that for hours, all I wanted to do was just gaze at the tree. It looked like an oak tree, tall and with many branches, and it seemed so real.

Toward the end of July, I moved back to Oklahoma City and moved in with my father and stepmother, who my father had married about two months before I left the Sapulpa nursing home. I had to wait for the authorization to go to the rehabilitation center in Virginia. The authorization came near the end of October, and I received the airline tickets from Gerald Davis.

My brother, Paul Howard, and I made plans to leave. At first, I had planned to go alone, but airline regulations said that someone had to accompany me. Paul Howard was just out of the Air Force and was not working at the time, so he accompanied me. I was anxious and nervous to know that I would soon be flying.

We drove to the airport, where I got into a special wheelchair, which was very narrow so that it could fit into the plane.

On the plane, my brother lifted me into my seat, and he sat beside me, in the window seat. I had to sit near the aisle because I was having a lot of trouble with my leg becoming stiff and not wanting to bend, so I had to sit where my leg would have enough room to stick straight out into the aisle. I began sliding down in the seat because it did not have the foam and sheepskin that I used in my wheelchair to keep me stationary. My brother helped push me back up into my seat, and I thanked him. But then I realized that in the process my urinary bag had somehow been pulled, and the tape that held it to my stomach had come slightly loose. It had started leaking.

"Oh, no," I thought, as I had a fleeting vision of the aircraft being flooded with a sea of urine.

I knew that I must keep calm. I got a towel out of my bag and put it between me and the seat, hoping to absorb the leakage. We got to Chicago, where some people got off or changed planes, but we stayed on our plane and waited for the takeoff to Washington, D.C. All the while, I sat there worried and anxious, fearful that I would be drenched with my own urine and badly embarrassed. We ate dinner on the plane, but I was careful to drink very little.

We arrived in Washington, D.C., around midnight, and the first thing we did was rush into an airport restroom, where Paul Howard helped me change my urine bag. I felt so relieved.

A man who looked like an important official spotted us and told us to hurry and get into a van that was designed for people in wheelchairs and that was to take us to the plane for the last leg of the trip. The plane was a small aircraft that held about twenty-five people.

It was late October, and it was freezing cold outside, windy and sleeting, with snow here and there on the ground. We got out of the van, with the man telling us all the while to hurry, please hurry. The other passengers were already on the plane and waiting for us to come aboard.

I looked up at the steep steps leading to the plane entrance. They were slick and icy. The man made motions as if he wanted to carry me up the steps, and I realized then that I had better make something clear to this man. Through Paul Howard, I told him that he must be very careful not to let anything hit my bottom because the skin was very sensitive and would tear and bleed easily.

We began our ascent up the steps, two big men carrying me. It was a slow process, and I did not want to look down. I was scared and cold, and it seemed as if we would never get aboard. At last, we were inside, and the men set me down in the front row and put my wheelchair underneath the seat, as they had done on the other plane.

With a sigh of relief that everything had gone all right, I settled into my seat and shortly began warming up. I looked out the window after we took off and saw the tall, white Washington Monument; I was fascinated by the red beam of light rotating around it. It was beautiful. I remember seeing a lake and cars becoming smaller and smaller as we rose higher into the air.

We landed near Fishersville sometime around one o'clock in the morning, and I began worrying about getting down those dreaded steps. It was a cold and windy night, and the steps still appeared very slick. They took my wheelchair down and then carried me down those steep steps, with me praying to God all the way.

I checked into the Woodrow Wilson Rehabilitation Center on October 30, 1979. It was much like the one back in Tulsa, as far as the living arrangements were concerned. I was assigned a hospital-like room in a hospital-like dormitory. When I first got there, I had meetings at long tables, around which people I presumed to be counselors asked me a lot of questions about why I had come to Virginia and what I wanted to do. After that, for a couple of weeks, I seemed to do a lot of waiting.

Finally, the physical therapists and occupational therapists began to examine me to assess my capabilities. There was a lot of poking and prodding to see what I could or could not feel, and there were tests to see what I could do with my hands. There were math tests that were almost the same as those I had done back home. Since the center was closed for the holidays, and since I could not return home, at Christmas I was moved into Rosehill Nursing Home, which was about a three-hour drive away. It was very new and modern, and most of the rooms were unoccupied. There was a Christmas party for a small group of us, at which I was chosen to be the New Year's Baby. I donned a diaper and, with balloons streaming from my wheelchair and blowing my party horn, made a grand entrance to a round of applause.

Back at the center after the holidays, I stayed in a hospital-type atmosphere called "Unit 2" for a couple of months, where I learned how to take care of my basic needs, such as dressing, bathing, and laundering clothes.

One afternoon, a nurse came in to see me, and I could see that she was excited about something. I noticed she had a picture that she wanted to show me. It was about two feet by three feet, and when she put it in front of me, I couldn't believe my eyes. There, in living color, was the tree from my strange dream back at Hillcrest! I was shocked to see that every line, every leafless branch, was exactly the same as I had dreamed. I hid my astonishment from the nurse and told her it was beautiful, knowing that if I said anything about my dream, she would not believe me.

Seeing the tree like this bothered me to such an extent that I decided to visit the school counselor the next morning. She greeted me in sign language as I wheeled myself into her office. She found my story to be very interesting; she never showed any trace of doubt and appeared to truly believe what I told her. She explained that that sort of occurrence has a name, though one that I can't recall, and said that it has happened before to other people. I felt much better when I left her office.

My days at the center soon settled into a sort of basic pattern centered around four buildings: the building in which I slept, the building in which I ate, the building in which I had physical therapy, and the building in which I went to school. The pattern was in effect Monday through Friday, and Saturdays and Sundays were free days. It had apparently been determined that my vocational training should be clerical, so my school hours mostly focused on math, typing, how to write business letters, and things like that.

A lot of the time, I did not feel I was doing very well. Once again, I had a communication problem because sign language was not used in the classrooms, and I did not always know what was being said. Interpreters were available and could be called in from time to time, whenever it was thought they were really needed, but I really needed someone with me all the time.

Sometimes I became so frustrated that I felt I couldn't stay, so I would leave and go back to my room before the class ended. I felt a lot of pressure, but I also knew that this was my chance and I must stick it out. I do not quite know how to explain how I felt. I only know that I was often frustrated and felt a lot of pressure. I did not feel that I was wasting my time, but neither did I feel that I was learning very much.

Now, looking back, I wish that I could have handled it better. I think I could have learned much more.

# 9

## Betty

I was very lonesome at the school in Virginia. The friends I made would often lose patience with me as I struggled to communicate with paralyzed hands. They would excuse themselves and walk away.

One day, I saw a pretty deaf girl sitting in the Deaf Project Building. She was reading a book. When our eyes met, she quickly and shyly looked away. I went back there for weeks, and this happened every time. I wanted her to notice me, but I couldn't think of a way to get her to.

One day, I moved closer and suddenly thought of a way. I happened to have an apple with me and, when she looked my way, I tossed it toward her. She instinctively caught it and gave me a big, pretty smile. We talked very briefly, and when it was time for class, we parted. I couldn't stop thinking about my new friend. We met again from time to time, talked more with each other, and became closer. Her name was Betty.

She told me that she had started her first day of training at WWRC on January 9, 1980. After dinner on that same day, she bumped into a deaf man she had met when she was there the summer before for an evaluation. He was on his way to deliver a magazine to me and asked her if she wanted to come along and meet me. He explained to her that I was deaf and paralyzed. She told him she really didn't understand what that meant, but she went with him. She told me she remembered seeing a hospital-type unit with many bedrooms and that she told the man she was concerned about seeing a man in his bedroom, in bed, and thought it would

Don and Betty.

not be proper. Again, he explained to her that I could not get out of bed because I was paralyzed. She continued with him but hesitated and stood by the doorway of my bedroom and stayed there as we were introduced. I remembered this encounter vaguely, as it had been some time ago, and gave her a big smile. She also told me that all those weeks in the Deaf Project Building, she was just pretending to read and was really interested in watching me.

When springtime came, we began to sit outside and talk in the warm sun. It was then that I noticed an amazing thing. About midway up her upper right arm, she had a tattoo. It was an image of the leafless tree with many branches—the very tree that I had dreamed about and that the nurse's son had drawn a picture of! I explained to Betty about my dream, and she was very interested in what I had to say. We decided to call the tree "the mystery tree," and we believed that it meant something special for both of us.

We would talk for hours about her life and my life, our personal stories, our likes and dislikes. It was so good to really talk with someone who was patient and who understood me. I also felt that

Betty needed to talk with me as badly as I needed to talk with her. She was someone who really cared, and I soon fell in love with her.

Before we met, Betty had experienced challenges far beyond just her hearing loss. Born two months premature and one of twins (six minutes apart), Betty stayed longer in the hospital. She was born hard of hearing, and as she grew, she began to labor with learning problems, seizures, and developmental disabilities. She struggled in school and was placed in a Special Education program and labeled "mentally retarded." She hated school and did not understand what was expected of her. They said she had dyslexia. Everything seemed to have a label.

Betty, who was darker in complexion than her twin and had long chestnut hair, felt that her family was whispering around her all the time. Her mom would be washing dishes at the sink and tell her to do something, but her voice, to Betty, was not understandable. If Betty asked someone to repeat what they said, she was immediately yelled at. The family was very impatient, it seemed to her, and angry when she did not understand right away. They would force her to say the word correctly, but not in a kind way. Thinking back, Betty felt that they must have thought her behavior was only to get attention. But she was glad, in a way, that she learned how to say the words because it helped her later in life.

When Betty was six years old, her parents tried to make her write her name, but she couldn't do it. She felt stuck. They beat her and made her stand on one foot for several hours while tied to the stair railing. They would bring back the paper and demand that she write her name. Again, she could not do it, and again they beat her and made her stand on one foot. This went on for several days. She finally wrote her name but it was backwards.

At age eight, she was forced to stay in the basement, isolated from the rest of the family. She would come upstairs to eat, but it felt like torture to her. Her mother watched her every move. When she did not follow all of her mother's impossible demands, Betty was beaten and sent back downstairs to the basement.

At age fifteen, Betty was removed from her home and placed in a foster home. Around that time, a teacher at school realized she had a hearing loss and started to teach her sign language. That was when she received her first hearing aids.

About eight months later, she went to Shalom, a therapeutic residential place for people with family and drug problems. There, they determined she was probably born with a moderate hearing loss and had a lot of damage to her eardrum due to many infections. She was at Shalom for four years, and she told me it was the first time in her life that she had love, understanding, and a better education. For the first time, Betty met a deaf girl like herself, who was also a student there, and she learned sign language and how to communicate. It was a new world.

When she graduated from Shalom, Betty went to Woodrow Wilson Rehabilitation Center, where we met. I felt I could gaze into those sparkling dark brown eyes forever, and Betty once told me that when I taught her sign language, she thought we spent so much time together signing we would run out of things to say, but we never did.

Betty was at the rehabilitation center to train for independent living and to work on a vocation. She frequently went home on weekends, and we began to work on the prospect of my visiting her there some weekend.

It was May 1980, and I had become friends with a deaf guy named Bruce. A group of us were sitting around talking in the cafeteria one day, and I asked Bruce if he could give me a ride in his pickup truck to Betty's home, which was about 105 miles from Fishersville. I was delighted when Bruce said he would help me get there as soon as he finished with his evaluations, and we set a time for two weeks later.

On the Thursday before the appointed weekend, I looked for Bruce but could not find him. On Friday I waited for him, but he did not show up. By Saturday, I was disappointed and depressed; Bruce had, of course, checked out and gone, leaving both Betty and I frustrated.

I had tried the only way I knew to get out of the school. No one else had a truck or van for me to travel in. So I came to the conclusion that I was stuck. I was sick of having to stay at the center all the time, never being able to leave because of my wheelchair. I was also sick of the rules and regulations and the strict atmosphere of the school. They wouldn't allow anyone to leave without their own transportation.

But Betty was very stubborn and began to rack her brain for a solution to the problem. She said she would help me get out. She came to me one day with the idea that we could at least take a cab somewhere. I stared at her in disbelief.

"How do you think we will do that," I asked.

"I can lift you into it," she replied.

I knew that she could not possibly lift me. I told her she was too small and thin and that she would have to get someone to help her.

She gave me a determined look and said, "I can do it."

She wasn't sure exactly how, but she felt she could learn to do it, and so we left with the idea that we would work on it.

A few days later, I had a sudden thought. Betty could push my wheelchair all the way back so that I was on my back on the floor or ground, then she could pull me out by grabbing me under the arms. We thought it worth a try and resolved to figure it out. The easiest place to test the theory was at the lake.

Every weekend, Betty and I would leave the center and go to a nearby lake that belonged to the school. It was about one and a half blocks away, so we could walk and she could push my wheelchair. A small sloping hill bordered the lake and was covered with rows and rows of green trees. At the base of the hill leading down to the lake, there was a small valley-like area that was somewhat secluded.

Sometimes we had great fun just rolling down the hill in my wheelchair, with Betty sitting on my lap and holding the long metal brakes on either side of the chair. Sometimes we would build a fire in the outdoor grill and cook and eat the hot dogs we brought along for lunch. Sometimes we would sunbathe in the hot afternoon sun and pour water from a jug over each other to keep cool. Always we had wonderful conversations on those outings, and often Betty would sit in my lap and we would hug and kiss.

The lakeside spot seemed the perfect place to practice the idea of her getting me out of, and back into, the wheelchair. The only problem was that the center's security personnel patrolled the lake area. They took exception to our using the outdoor grill without express permission. They also took exception to Betty's sitting in my lap and to the romantic petting. They were certain to take exception to our efforts toward getting me out of the wheelchair.

We reasoned that if we timed the security car just right as it made its rounds and could reach the bottom of the hill without being seen, then we would be free to conduct our little experiment. And it worked. We decided the best way to start would be to pull the wheelchair back all the way to the ground and then back to an upright position. We wanted to make sure that she could do that much before we tried to get me completely out of the chair. The first time, it was awkward and we had to try several times in several different positions until we finally got me back upright.

We returned to the school with a feeling of excitement about having been able to accomplish the first step, but also with a tinge of anxiety about the next step. We continued our visits to the lake, practicing until we were able to lean the chair back and smoothly get it back up again. Eventually, we were able to accomplish the feat of getting me out of and back into the wheelchair.

On one particular visit to the lake, Betty got me on my back and lay beside me for about an hour. It was very peaceful. We looked at the sky together, and I relished the feel of the grass on my arms. I was able to recall how, as a boy, I had constantly walked through the cool grass in my bare feet, a sensation that I had not been able to experience for many, many years. When we felt it was time to leave, Betty tried to get the wheelchair up to the upright position, but she was not able to do so. She strained and pushed, but to no avail. She could not quite understand what was wrong.

Then she realized that we had forgotten the extension bars for the back of my wheelchair. This was not an electric-type wheelchair, and each day a set of extension bars was connected to the back of my wheelchair to help support my back and head. We had removed them in order to make traveling to the lake a little easier, and we had forgotten to bring them along. If I had been lying on flat ground, I think Betty could have raised me without the bars, but I was lying at an angle on the slope of the hill. Without the extension bars, Betty had nothing to grab for leverage.

We were in a quandary as to what we should do, and we felt a sense of urgency because we were afraid the security patrol might come back at any minute and catch us in our predicament. Matters became worse when the wheelchair began to slide down the slope of the hill. Every time Betty tried to move the chair, it slid down a little further. We were getting nowhere. We tried to think clearly and not panic.

At last, I had an idea when I spotted a water faucet rising a few feet out of the ground at just about the top of the hill. Luckily, we had brought along a rope in the bag on the back of my chair for an emergency. I instructed Betty how to tie one end of the rope to the faucet and the other end to the back of my chair. She was shaking because she was so nervous, but she calmed down enough to do as I said. It seemed to take a long time for her to do it. Slowly, ever so slowly, she pulled the rope tighter and tighter, tying it repeatedly as the wheelchair moved inch by inch up the hill. The stretch of rope became shorter and shorter, until the chair was brought back to level ground and into an upright position. We both heaved a big sigh of relief, which changed to excitement when we realized we had attained a big portion of our goal. We felt that we had proven to ourselves that we could work out problems and handle emergencies if they should arise.

Sometimes the school would take us in a bus downtown to go shopping. We would look at all the different kinds of clothes. I particularly noticed the girls' clothes, so beautiful, with lace on them. I had never seen Betty wear such feminine clothes. I told her that

I really liked them, and after that, I noticed that she began wearing more of them. I thought she looked so pretty, and I think she began feeling more like a girl. After shopping, we would return to our classes, Betty to her carpentry class and me to my clerical and business-type classes. After classes ended, we would usually meet again, rush down the hall to eat at the cafeteria, then head for the dorms, laughing together and acting silly.

Then the school decided to send Betty for her independent living training. The training was done in a nearby cottage, in which the student was to live alone for one week, cooking, cleaning, and caring for herself without help.

Betty wanted to invite me to supper one night, but the counselor said, "No, not unless you have a staff member present."

Betty was upset about the rule, and I suggested that we go ahead and let the staff member come, then lock her up in a closet while we had our privacy. We had a good laugh over the idea, but we knew that we couldn't do anything like that. We would have to follow the rules.

When I arrived at the cottage, Betty greeted me at the door, and I gave her a gift. The staff member was already there and stood, watching our every move. But I got the feeling that she was as disgusted with the rules as we were because, after a while, she surprised us by saying that she had to go and would be back later. We were glad to see her go but were also a little worried that the counselor, who we really liked, might get in trouble if anyone found out that the chaperone had left. Betty had cooked liver and onions and banana pudding, my favorites. She served the meal and it was wonderful, then we talked for a while.

Later I asked, "What will I do if the security guard comes and finds us alone together?"

We really were concerned because it seemed the security guards were always around checking on things.

Betty looked across the empty dishes at me and said, "Simple. Just hide in the bathroom."

Suddenly the doorbell rang and we both jumped. With Betty's residual hearing, she had recognized the sound, and her reaction caused me to jump, even though I had not heard anything. The table lurched, and dishes scattered. I took off for the bathroom, but the doorway was too narrow for me to go through. I tried a closet and another room, without luck. I finally got through the bedroom door. There was no good place to hide in there, so I went into a corner and sat. Betty came running in after me with my share of the dirty dishes, which she piled into my lap. Then she covered me and the dishes from head to toe with a blanket. I stayed very still, practically holding my breath.

After a short time, Betty opened the front door. With relief, she saw the face of a friend, who only stayed briefly. As soon as Betty gave the all-clear, I came out, she cleaned the dirty dishes off of me, and we laughed at how funny the episode must have looked. We talked until about ten o'clock, when I decided I should get back to my dorm. We hugged and I quietly snuck out into a light rain. The chaperone never came back.

I was never given training in independent living. It was different for people with disabilities like mine. I might have been able to handle a few simple chores or some simple cooking, but there was no way I could live alone like that without a certain amount of assistance.

# 10

## Chincoteague

In August 1980, Betty and I decided to go on a trip from the rehabilitation center, which was near the West Virginia state line, to Chincoteague Island, a small island off the peninsula on the eastern side of Chesapeake Bay, just south of the Maryland state line. Betty suggested the place; she had been there before.

The vacation was to be for a week, and the staff at the center had to approve the trip. It was difficult, but I eventually received the necessary permission. We understood that Betty would be the only one to take care of me on the trip, and the school training nurse spent about a month instructing her on how to do it. She had to learn everything, such as how to bathe me, change my clothes and urinary collector, get me into bed, and do a certain amount of physical therapy.

Perhaps I should explain the nature of our relationship at that time. Betty and I had an understanding that she would stay with me when we traveled, not only because we loved each other, but also because it was absolutely necessary. It was not a physical relationship in the sense that one might think, because such was not really possible. Normal male sexual responses and normal sexual gratification were not possible for me after the accident that had broken my neck. For her own reasons, Betty did not require or desire a relationship of this nature. Although we unquestionably found pleasure in touching and hugging, this was a manifestation of our deeper relationship of trust, love, understanding, and mutual help that had developed over the past several months.

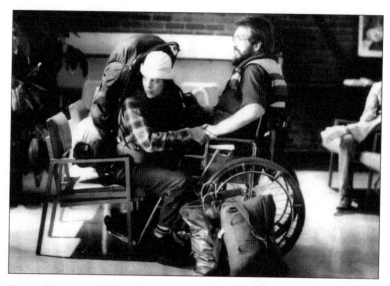

Don and Betty get ready to leave for Chincoteague.

Right after we first met, Betty often became frustrated with me because I could not share my feelings. I had never shared my feelings with anyone all my life. When I recalled the time my mother died and how heartbroken my father and siblings had been, I remembered feeling nothing, really. Perhaps, in a way, I had loved my mother, but I did not really know her. I did not really have a relationship or communicate with her. As Helen Keller said, blindness can cut a person off from things, but deafness can cut a person off from people.

I thought back to the girlfriend I had in high school and realized how superficial and meaningless that relationship was compared to the one that Betty and I shared. Betty and I had deep, sincere, honest communication, and I felt that Betty was responsible for bringing the meaning of the word "relationship" into my life.

We took a commercial bus to Chincoteague Island. When we got to the bus station, we thought the driver was really mean because he refused to help me onto the bus. Betty was very upset by this but, determined that the trip would go on, she asked the center's security staff member, who had accompanied us to the bus station, to help carry my wheelchair up the steps and into the bus. The ride lasted all day, from seven o'clock in the morning until seven that night. Although Chincoteague Island is almost due east of Fishersville, we followed a route that went in a southeasterly direction to Norfolk, so that we crossed Chesapeake Bay at a relatively narrow point and arrived on the eastern peninsula by means of a network of bridges and tunnels.

The bus dropped us off near the island, and we waited long enough to eat the lunch we had brought. Then Betty tried to push my wheelchair along the roadside while we attempted to hitchhike. The first car that passed stopped for us. Luckily, it was a van. The driver opened the back of the van for us and tried to help Betty lift me into the back, but she was not strong enough.

As we mulled over the problem, an old Chevy pulled up and a pleasant-looking man got out. He was very friendly and helpful, and he and Betty got me into the back of the van.

He questioned me with his eyes as if to ask, "All right?"

I nodded and smiled and, before he left, Betty took a picture of us. Then she jumped up into the van and sat on my lap as the woman shut the back doors of the van. Betty handed the woman the address of the cottage in Chincoteague where she had reservations. We drove straight to it, and the woman pulled up beside the cottage and stopped. After someone on the premises helped us out of the van, we thanked the woman and she left.

Inside the cottage, an elderly woman gave us our key and showed us to our room. We were very tired. We went straight to bed and fell fast asleep the minute our heads hit the pillows. The next morning, Betty woke me up by tugging on my shoulders.

"Time to get up," she said.

She gave me a sponge bath as I lay on the bed and then dressed me and got me into my chair. After we ate breakfast, we went outside for a walk and looked around at all the other cottages and restaurants. It was a Saturday, and only a few people were out. The surroundings looked like a fishing village, and a strong smell of fish permeated the air. A huge pile of clam or oyster shells sat outside a nearby restaurant, and Betty decided it would be interesting to go inside. As we entered, a huge lobster stared at us from inside a glass case. It was the biggest one I had ever seen in my life, and its claws were as big as my hands. The man behind the counter pulled it out of the case so that we could touch it. At first I was afraid to, but when I saw that its claws were wrapped tight, I went ahead.

We went outside and walked on, looking around at all the interesting places, people, and boats.

Suddenly Betty screamed with delight, "Meagan and Eric!"

We saw two of her good friends, whom she knew from the Shalom, driving up in a car with a sailboat. They were on their way home when we ran into them, so we talked briefly and they drove on.

We spotted a souvenir shop and couldn't resist going in for a look. The hats drew Betty's attention. She stood before the mirror and tried on hat after hat, wrinkling her nose with each one, a look of dissatisfaction clouding her face. She tried some on me; ultimately, one looked good to her, but only after she had turned it around backwards on my head. She smiled her approval, stepping back with her hands on her hips, while the salesman looked at us as if we were crazy. We bought the hat, left, and began walking toward another beach.

It was soon dark, and we thought it best to go back to the cottage. Betty stuck out her thumb, hoping for a ride, but none came. After a long wait, a car stopped. After we realized there was no way for me to get into the car, we declined. The man and woman insisted, gesturing with their arms an offer of a ride, and I could clearly see that they were drunk.

They finally drove away, and soon a park ranger in a pickup truck pulled up near us. He helped us into the truck and took us back to our cottage. We thanked him, and he told us he would like to come back tomorrow to take us on a ride and show us the island. We happily agreed.

The following morning, the ranger arrived, as he had promised. He took us to a harbor where a large boat was docked and ready to take passengers on a tour. I asked the tour guide about my wheelchair, but he indicated that it was fine. There was an admission charge, but the tour guide said Betty and I could board for free. The long ramp onto the boat was very narrow and Betty had a hard time pushing me up, but we made it aboard and maneuvered our way to about the middle of the upper deck, where we found a good place to sit. Betty sat on a wooden bench she had made to put on my lap so that she could easily sit there without causing me discomfort.

We watched as the boat moved away from the shore and the blue waves rolled by. We traveled a long way out into the ocean until we could no longer see land. The waves lapped high on the sides of the boat while we threw pieces of bread into the air and watched as the seagulls dove to catch them, perfectly, never missing. The boat trip took about an hour.

When we returned to shore and went down the ramp, our ranger friend was there, waiting for us. We loaded into his pickup again, and he drove us out to see the wild ponies. The road wound around the island, and before we knew it, we were in the middle of many ponies of similar size, but all different colors. Some were so close to the truck we could almost reach out and touch them.

After seeing the ponies, the ranger took us back to the cottage, and we thanked him very much for all his generous help. Then we walked to the grocery store to buy some food, went back to the cottage, and began planning for the next day.

The next morning, we got up and readied ourselves. The old woman who owned the cottage gave us a big bucketful of stinking fish heads and suggested that we take a net and go crabbing. So we did. We had no trouble hitchhiking. Very quickly a van slowed and came to a stop, and a tall, balding man got out and helped me into the back. He was very friendly. Betty was a good lip-reader, and she told me that the man said he had a son who also had a broken neck, and he owned a store not too far from the beach. After he dropped us off at the beach and drove away, Betty excitedly got out her camera and aimed it. But I saw a frown fill her face and the camera come slowly down to rest at her side.

"No film," she said. She was so disappointed.

"Can buy film?" she signed.

''Far," I replied, but before I knew it, we were back by the side of the road with our thumbs out.

Without much delay, another van stopped to pick us up. A woman in her thirties got out, and I think she was afraid to say anything when she realized we were deaf. But she kept smiling pleasantly as she silently helped me into her van.

Betty said "store" clearly, and the woman understood.

She dropped us off at a little store with taffy winding away in a window. We watched her drive away, still smiling. We hurried through the store and grabbed some film. When we turned around, we were surprised to see the tall, balding man again. Apparently we had come to his store.

We grinned and said hello to him on our way out.

We knew he must have been surprised to see us, since he had just dropped us off at the beach eight miles away.

It wasn't long before another van stopped and a young boy got out.

He waved to us to "come on," and it was obvious that he was a bit tipsy. He beamed at us and swayed a little from side to side.

Betty was hesitant, but we went ahead and got in. As soon as we were settled in the van, the boy offered us some beer.

"No thanks," we shook our heads.

We arrived at the beach without incident.

Betty began pushing my wheelchair along the beach, and I told her that I was worried about my wheels getting stuck in the sand.

She said, "Don't worry," and steered me over to a black mat on the sand.

The mat was a kind of rubberized canvas strip tacked down all along the beach near the water. It was a special path for people in wheelchairs! I thought it was a great idea. The island gets a lot of wheelchair visitors, which probably accounted for the special mat walkway as well as for the wheelchair ramps I saw everywhere.

We had some bread with us to feed the seagulls. I tossed a piece into the air, and before I knew it, there were many, many birds above our heads. They dove and swooped gracefully in the air, and we had so much fun watching them. We threw bread until it was almost gone.

Suddenly, a movement in the air caught our attention. A man casting a fishing line nearby had accidentally hooked a seagull. It came down with a thud and scrambled helplessly on the ground, dragging a crumpled wing. Betty's happy face turned to one of anger and hurt.

She turned to me and signed, "Stop! No more bread. Let them fly away!"

The seagulls flew off, and we saw a ranger pick up the hurt bird and walk away. The man who had hurt the bird seemed to be apologizing over and over to the ranger. Betty was so upset by what she had seen that we had to sit quietly by the water for a while until she felt better. As I sat and watched people of all descriptions going by, I thought about Betty's love for nature and living things: the way she would study a June-bug for hours or sit patiently watching a spider weave its web. The bird was hurt, and so was she.

When Betty was feeling better, a man walked up and showed us a baby shark he had caught. I was surprised to see one so tiny. Then Betty decided that we should sunbathe for a while, and she tipped my chair backwards so that I lay on my back looking up at the sky, with my feet sticking straight up into the air. I must have looked ridiculous.

Later, we decided to try to catch some crabs. A ranger came along and tried to show us the proper way. I watched doubtfully as he demonstrated in pantomime how it should be done. He suggested that we go down to the river about a mile from the ocean, and so we did. When we got to the river, I stared at the three feet of water, wondering how we could ever catch a crab.

Crabbing in Chincoteague.

"This isn't going to work," I said to Betty, but she wanted to try anyway.

She took the strings that we had brought and tied one end to the armrest of my wheelchair and the other end to one of the fish heads we had been carrying around with us. She threw the fish head as far as she could, out into the water. I sat and waited, thinking how stupid this all was.

Suddenly the line jerked in my hands, and Betty told me to reel it in very slowly. She crouched nearby with the net and, when the crab got near enough, in her excitement, she pounced on it so hard with the net that she caused the crab to fly over our heads and land on the road behind us. It ambled jerkily quite a ways down the road, and Betty ran after it, laughing, until she caught up with it and threw it in her bucket.

Our first attempt, and already we had caught one. I decided to stop being a skeptic. This was really fun. We did it again and again until we caught five crabs altogether. When the sun started lazily down, we decided we should go before it got dark. Betty felt sorry for the crabs, so one by one, she put them gently back into the water.

We made it back to the road and started thumbing once again. Yet another van stopped. A woman was driving, and the man with her helped lift me into the van. They dropped us off at a small town, and it was getting dark by that time. We continued on toward the cottage.

Betty stopped and pointed toward an outdoor movie theater that was showing *The Blue Lagoon*. We decided to stay and watch it. Although the movie had already started, we paid and went in. We enjoyed watching the pictures even if we couldn't hear the words. Suddenly I thought I smelled fish—yes, it was the distinct odor of fish. The bucket of stinky fish heads we had used for crab bait was still dangling underneath my chair

"Oh well, really nothing we can do now," I said. "Anyway, the movie seems more real."

We both laughed as Betty signed, "P-U."

Before the week ended, as a sort of final treat, I invited Betty to go to a seafood restaurant. She was excited by the invitation because we had never eaten seafood, and we decided we wanted to try it. The restaurant was dark. The waitress showed us to our table as we blinked to adjust our eyes to the dimly lit room and the single little candle on the table. Upon opening the huge and fancy-looking menus, I was greeted by many large words that looked foreign and prices that were equally large. I did not know what to order, and I asked Betty what she would like. She only shrugged her shoulders and told me to decide.

I finally pointed to something and signed to her "This looks good, what do you think?"

She said that it was fine. So we ordered, but we did not really know what we had ordered except for soft shell crabs.

After a while, the waitress appeared with two heavily laden plates, placed them in front of us, and disappeared into the darkness. I carefully tested each item on my plate with a fork, trying to get a feel for whatever it was we had ordered. I hit something hard in the middle of my plate, pushed in with the fork, and suddenly something that looked like a bunch of legs came at me. I was so startled that I tipped backwards in my chair and very nearly landed on my back on the restaurant floor. Betty could not contain herself—she broke out with laughter. I had to laugh right along with her—to almost think that I had been attacked by my dinner! When we regained our composure enough to try to eat our dinner, I noticed that Betty loved hers, but I wasn't enjoying the taste of mine at all. I gave up and focused my attention on the wine.

Needless to say, I was feeling pretty good by the time we were ready to leave. Too soon, the vacation was over. It probably sounds like a very simple holiday, but I never thought such a holiday could be possible for me.

However, there was yet a price to pay. After we returned home by bus, the nurse had to check me before I could attend classes again. She told me that I absolutely could not return to classes for one month because I had a bedsore on my buttocks. I was very disappointed. I had to be placed on a stretcher instead of in my wheelchair. I went from bed to stretcher, and back again, that entire month.

One day, the nurse told me the sore was not getting better and that the only thing to do to help it heal was to give it sunlight. She explained that the artificial light of a sunlamp would not work and that I must lay outside with my butt exposed to the sun (and, naturally, to all passers-by). The only place to do this was the grassy area in the middle of the U-shaped space formed by the girls' dormitory. There I lay, day in and day out, with the girls going by to classes. How embarrassing! Of course, there was a sheet over me, so that only my butt showed. Apparently it was nothing to see—people did not stand around staring, although Betty and a few others I knew came by to talk.

Thanksgiving arrived—the holiday that had always made me feel nervous and uncomfortable. But this year, I was determined that Thanksgiving would be different. This year, I had special plans. Betty and I were to have Thanksgiving dinner at the home of a woman who worked as a housemother at the center and whom we both liked very much. Then both of us would spend the night in a downtown Fishersville hotel and travel the next day to the Shalom, where we would live while the living quarters at the center were closed for the holidays. More than this, I would be carrying with me an engagement ring that I hoped to present to Betty at the appropriate moment.

We spent the day at the woman's house, where she served a beautiful dinner. Later, she dropped us off at the old hotel, which was about ten stories tall, had brown brick and white trim, and was near the bus station from which we would leave the next day. On the way to the hotel, I kept feeling in my coat pocket to make sure the ring was still there. I couldn't wait to surprise Betty with it.

After our friend left, I noticed that there was no way I could get my wheelchair up the steps and through the main door of the hotel and that I would have to go up a small hill and through the door. I asked Betty to wait in the basement while I went up in the elevator to the lobby and made the necessary arrangements.

I then went back down to the basement to get Betty. Our room was on the seventh floor. By now Betty was experienced and knew what she had to do, so she began helping me get ready for bed. She hung up my coat. I grinned and swallowed hard, knowing that she did not suspect what lay inside my pocket, and hoped that she would accept the gift. We talked for a long time, but when it got close to ten o'clock, I decided that it was now or never. I asked her to look inside the pocket of my coat.

"Why?" she asked.

"Just look," I said.

She dug inside the pocket, pulled out the small box, and opened it. When she saw the ring, her eyes widened, she smiled at me, and then she hugged and kissed me with excitement.

"Will you accept," I signed, already knowing the answer.

We had discussed wedding plans that night, although nothing real or definite.

"And I will dance you around and around in my wheelchair," I told Betty.

The next day, we caught the first available bus for Winchester. It was a cold morning. The bus driver did not want to help lift me into the bus, so a helpful stranger offered to assist. Someone folded up my wheelchair and placed it in the luggage bin underneath the bus while the stranger and Betty lifted me into one of the front seats of the bus.

Somehow, in the process of the lifting, my pants got pulled down and I happened to "moon" all the passengers. Betty managed to get my pants pulled back up and then sat behind me and held on to me so I wouldn't fall forward onto the floor. Another embarrassing moment. But I was used to those, and Betty had to get used to them too. We both laughed about it; she helped me to take such things lightly.

Still, I decided to buy some suspenders.

# 11

## Learning to Live

Betty and I decided we would stay in Virginia after we both finished our training at the rehabilitation center. Betty's training was scheduled to be completed after mine, so we asked that arrangements be made so that we could finish together. However, employment opportunities for me seemed to be few in Virginia. I sent out a few applications seeking a job as a general clerk, but nothing came of them. There seemed to be more available to Betty, but nothing for me.

Both my counselor in Fishersville and Gerald Davis, my counselor at the Vocational Rehabilitation office back in Tulsa, decided that I would have better opportunities in Tulsa. I asked Betty if she would come back to Tulsa with me, and she happily agreed to do so.

On Valentine's Day of 1981, Betty and I flew to Tulsa. Judy and George Peknik met us at the airport. They took us to their home, where we stayed for about three weeks while George hunted for a place for us to live. In early March, he found us a duplex at 14th and Denver, near downtown Tulsa. It was an ordinary style apartment; there were no special features for the disabled. In fact, we had to lay down a door as a ramp in order to enter the apartment but there was no rug, which was good. There was also a convenience grocery store nearby.

A couple of months went by, and we both struggled with being unemployed. Gerald Davis and the Vocational Rehabilitation office in Tulsa knew that Betty was returning with me, and they helped her find a job. Although Betty's training at the center was princi-

Don.

pally in woodworking, in May she got a job with Telex Corporation, a computer products manufacturing company. Betty's work mostly involved working at a table, with a group of other women, assembling computer parts and instruments.

One day that summer, Betty asked me if I wanted to go with her the next day to see a movie called *Where the Red Fern Grows*, which was showing at the Park Lane Theater. I said I would love to go, but I asked her how we would get there. She replied that I could ride in my wheelchair and she would ride alongside on her bicycle.

I signed, "I don't think possible. Too far."

But she insisted that we could and that it would be a lot of fun. The first feature started shortly after noon, so I warned her that we would need to leave early in the morning because it would take a long time to get there.

The next morning, Betty, Sammy, and I left the apartment at seven o'clock. Sammy was her bird and she wanted to bring him along, so she strapped his cage onto the luggage rack over the rear wheel of her bicycle. I brought along my battery recharger in case my wheelchair batteries got low.

We started out down Riverside Drive on the biking and jogging trail between the street and the river. We watched the water and observed the trees along the riverbank. Birds flew about, and occasionally a rabbit would dart out and then disappear. Betty was happy and excited; her bicycle wove back and forth across the trail as she talked to me with her fingers. Sammy hung on tightly to his swinging perch, and we went merrily along. When it was time to turn away from the river, we went east on 48th Street so we could travel through residential areas and avoid too much heavy traffic.

About ten o'clock, we began looking for water because the sun had risen high in the sky and it was becoming hotter. Betty motioned for me to follow as she headed toward a lady who was watering her lawn with a garden hose. With her partial speech and gestures, Betty asked the lady to squirt us with water to cool us off. The lady understood and she soaked us thoroughly. We thanked her and went on our way. We came across a large lot with tall, sun-browned grass and a fence and a couple of horses. We stopped to pet a big white horse, and he seemed to enjoy the attention we gave him.

About an hour later, it was time again to look for more water. This time we spotted a man with a hose. He, too, was kind enough to give us a drink and douse us with his spray. We also asked for directions to the movie theater, and he told us it was not very much further. Still, we were concerned about getting to the movie on time and thought we had better hurry. Also, Betty was worried about Sammy being hot, so she took out her red blanket and gently covered his cage to shade him from the sun's rays.

We reached Yale Avenue, a very busy street, and had to wait until the heavy traffic cleared before we could cross. When we reached the other side, we both heaved sighs of relief. Then we went on to Sheridan Road, spotted the movie theater, bought our tickets, and rushed in, just in time for the movie. A nice man brought up a chair so that Betty could sit beside me. During the movie, I kept my battery charger plugged in so we could be ready for the trip home. We munched popcorn and drank cokes. Betty already knew the story because a friend had told her about it, so she explained it to me as we watched the actors' lips move on the screen.

When the movie was over, we tried to decide what we could do with the remainder of the afternoon. I suggested the water slide nearby, and it made me feel good to see Betty's face light up at my suggestion. I found a place to sit and watch while Betty had a delightful time zooming down the long slide into the water. She must have gone down fifteen times, and I had just as much fun watching her do it as if I were doing it myself.

After that, we went to a pizza place in the area for some dinner. While we ate our pizza, I made sure that my chair's battery was being recharged. We talked and laughed and had a very nice time, but when I noticed that the sun was beginning to set, I suggested that we leave.

I asked her if she had a flashlight, and she said, "Yes."

We started on our way. Sammy seemed so tired. The darkness soon closed in around us, and Betty constantly looked back at me to make sure I was okay. Whenever a car drove up behind me, she would shine her flashlight on me so that the driver could see me. But she was holding the light too high, its brightness was blinding me so that I couldn't see where I was going, and I would weave back and forth on the street. I finally got her attention and told her that she was blinding me. She apologized and promised to shine the light lower.

It was getting close to midnight when we arrived at Riverside Drive. All of a sudden, my wheelchair refused to move.

"Oh no! What's happened?" I thought to myself.

After Betty investigated, she discovered that my battery had fallen off. She ran back and tried to lift the battery, but it was too heavy for her.

After ten minutes of waiting, we were able to signal a passing car for help. The car pulled into a nearby driveway, and a man got out and came over to see what was wrong. He helped put the battery back on my chair. I tested it, and it seemed to be alright. We were relieved. We traveled on, but I was getting very tired, and my eyelids were getting heavy. I was almost to the point of dozing off when I hit a small ditch, which jolted me back to life. Betty asked me what was wrong, and I explained that I had almost fallen asleep.

She grinned and signed, "Wake up!"

We arrived home around one o'clock in the morning. Betty went in and lit a candle (for romance, she said) and placed Sammy's cage on the table next to it. She suggested that we eat something, and she made some light soup. As we ate, I told her to look at Sammy. He was tired and was barely hanging onto his ladder. I told her that his little legs would have big muscles on them from diligently hanging onto his perch for so long a trip. She burst into laughter.

We talked about the day and all the fun we had, and we counted up the miles—twenty-eight. I thought about how, for most people, it would have been a quick car ride to the theater, the pizza parlor, and back, but for us it was a full day's adventure.

Also that summer, one Saturday afternoon in July, I took another trip in my wheelchair that turned out to be rather frightening. Betty had gone shopping with a friend, and I was alone in the apartment. I became very restless, so I thought I would go out for a walk. When I got to the vicinity of 11th Street and Columbia, I was quite a ways from home and found myself in a deserted industrial area. It was all strange to me, and at times I stopped to look around. It was also very hot. I came to a bumpy area that I could not get around, so I decided to cross the railroad tracks and continue on. However, the thin wheel of my chair somehow got caught between the ties of the track. I tried repeatedly to wedge myself out, but try as I might, I could not. Sweat poured down my face and my back. I tried calling for help, but I knew my voice was weak from the heat. I tried waving my arms until I was too weak to lift them but nobody was around to hear or see me. I had no idea whether a train might come along at any minute. Nervous and scared, I sat on the tracks for what felt like an hour, wondering how I would get out of this.

At last, a pickup truck appeared. With a burst of energy, I frantically waved my arms. The man stopped and spoke to me from the truck. I gestured that I could not hear. He spoke again; again I gestured. Then he got out, came over, and became aware of my predicament. He lifted the chair and pushed me to freedom. I thanked him as best I could. Worn out from the strain and the heat and unable to think straight, I made my way to the nearest service station and managed to get someone to understand my request for water. I drank and drank, and poured some over my head. The man quickly brought me more and even brought me a free pop.

He wrote a note: "Where did you come from?"

I wrote back: "14th and Denver."

His eyes widened. I then went to a church a few blocks away, where a deaf friend worked. He was cleaning and preparing the church for the next day's services, and I stayed an hour or so chatting with him in sign language and then started on the long trip back home. When I got home, I had quite a story to tell Betty.

Now that Betty had a regular job at Telex, she found her responsibilities had doubled. She already had what practically was a full-time job taking care of a man who couldn't get out of bed without her help. Furthermore, she still had some emotional problems she had carried since childhood. She was under a great deal of stress at this time, and in August she asked me to move out. We had lived together for eight months. I went to live at Murdock Villa, a 144-unit, five-story, accessible apartment complex in Tulsa named for Aliene Murdock, who established the Recreation Center for the Physically Limited and who was a lifelong advocate for people with disabilities.

I moved the first week in August, and that month was a bad one in my life. I had a lot of problems the first few days because I had no regular provider (someone to help take care of me). It was hard to find someone. Each apartment had a panic button, but it was for use only in emergencies and not for things like getting out of bed and other routine needs.

At first, Jimmy, a deaf friend of mine who also lived at Murdock Villa, tried to help take care of me. Jimmy tried, but he had some developmental disabilities and, well, let me put it this way, it was never boring to have him around. One time, he tried to fix something in the bathroom sink with a hammer and busted the entire sink. Another time, Jimmy attempted to cook a frozen dinner by putting it in the oven, and it expanded to three times its original size. He also broke a framed granite award hanging on the wall when he lifted his arm to change the sheets. Jimmy really was a tender soul, and it upset him when these things happened, but he wasn't cut out for housekeeping work. At times things went missing, and when he was reprimanded, Jimmy would bang his head against the wall.

I set out to look for caregivers and had a succession of different people who did not work out for one reason or another. Some days no one would come, and I would lie in bed all day. Finally, in the fall, I found a dependable provider. Her name was Jewel.

Then in spring 1981, Vocational Rehabilitation told me they might have found a position for me with Lowrance Electronics, an electronics assembly plant. Gerald Davis was very optimistic about it. One day in June, Gerald and Kirby Hodges, his intern, put me in the back of Gerald's old pickup truck. With Kirby clutching onto the side of my wheelchair as we faced backwards, and the wind whipping through our hair, we slowly bumped down 11th Street from downtown Tulsa all the way to east Tulsa. I couldn't help smiling with excitement, thinking about my interview. Mr. Laenger, a rehabilitation engineer from Tulsa Rehabilitation Center, also went with us. When we arrived, we met our interpreter, Jennie Koons.

We went on a tour of the plant in an effort to identify jobs that might be adapted to my capabilities, and people asked me if I could do this and that. We were uncertain whether I could perform any of the available jobs in a productive manner, but Lowrance agreed to hire me on a trial basis. After a little time and with the help of one of their industrial engineers and Mr. Laenger, who fabricated special assembly-assist devices for me, Lowrance was apparently satisfied with my performance and hired me on a permanent basis.

My position was as an electromechanical assembly worker. I felt so proud that I was supporting myself. My second dream had come true. My first paycheck was a symbol of my ability to make my way in the world and to show that I was not dependent on anyone else to pay my way.

At Lowrance, we made "transducers," a kind of radar unit that was installed on boats. A screen showed a cone-shaped display of an image with squiggly lines that indicated any fish the device detected under the water and, depending on the length of those lines, you could tell how big the fish were.

My job consisted of putting a nut on a spinning bolt that rotated on a turntable. I could do this with the aid of a special hand brace. I would let it run down on the spinner about halfway until it connected, and then I'd throw it in a box. This, along with the rest of the unit, would go to the buyer. I felt I was doing something useful. I enjoyed my job, and I became better and faster at it as the years went by.

However, things at work weren't always enjoyable. Sometimes even small things could become major obstacles for me. For example, some employees would laugh or stare rudely at me while I tried to do my job, or it would become a complete struggle just to get a coin into the slot in the vending machine in the lunchroom.

It was during one of these "junk food" machine struggles that an angel came into my life. Connie Foster was the switchboard operator at Lowrance, and she sat at the desk at the end of a long hallway, at the building's entrance, that had a brown-and-white speckled tile floor and that was lined with pictures of colorful fish. She was, for me, the only bright spot in the otherwise cold, windowless, government-style building. When Connie walked up to the food machine that day, not only did my life change, but so did hers.

She said to me, "May I help you?"

I tried to show her what I needed. After a while, she figured out that not only could I not use my hands very well, but I was also deaf. I motioned to her to help me get a card out of the pack that I carried, and I gave it to her. It was one of many that I always carried with me and that I got from the Tulsa Speech and Hearing Association (TSHA). On the back of this card, symbols showed the alphabet in sign language. Connie took one look, and she was hooked. She began practicing every day.

I was so excited that someone at my job was interested in communicating with me. I was even more thrilled when she told me she was taking sign classes through TSHA. Each day, she practiced with me more and more, and communication became easier between the two of us. She was the only one at work who could sign with me. With everyone else, I had to write notes with a pen or pencil in my mouth, which was painstaking and tedious.

I worked every weekday but left a little early if I had to catch the lift bus. For about six months after I started my job, George Peknik had taken me to work every morning in his van, and he picked me up every afternoon and took me home, as arranged through Vocational Rehabilitation Services. Then I began using a special bus equipped with a lift for wheelchairs, the lift bus, which was maintained by the Metropolitan Tulsa Transit Authority (the city bus lines). To use this service, appointments had to be made ahead of time every day.

For most of the time I was at Lowrance, I had to rely on the lift bus for transportation. Many times it was late getting me to work, and this was extremely frustrating for me. I told Connie about it, and she called them to let them know how I felt, since I was unable to use the phone. They said that they had to pick up several other people and that they could do nothing about it. It was a helpless feeling. I continued to arrive late to work.

The looks and jeers from a small group of people at work became worse. I tolerated it as long as I could but after a time decided I needed help with it, and I was grateful I could go to Connie and ask her for help. She went right to the human resources office and took care of it. She was becoming more than just an advocate. She was, indeed, a friend.

The day I knew I could always count on Connie was the day she noticed I truly needed help and was there for me. She noticed that my colostomy bag was full and needed to be emptied. She came to me and asked if she could help. She followed me into the men's restroom, and even though some people seemed shocked, she walked right in and helped me empty the bag. I was always so grateful when she did this for me many times thereafter. Just knowing she was there gave me the peace of mind to be able to do my job without needless worry.

It was not always work around Lowrance. We also had fun. When Halloween rolled around each year, our company had a costume contest. One year, Connie went to great lengths to dress me up like a train. She cut up a refrigerator box and got two car headlights and her dad's engineer hat. By the time she was finished, I had won first place and a prize of fifty dollars.

Another Halloween, I put my electric wheelchair in coast and signed, "Help me!"

Connie couldn't figure out what was wrong. She thought I couldn't breathe. I pointed to my leg, and she saw a big plastic spider I had put there, and she jumped, scared to death. I thought that was pretty funny.

Most of the people at Lowrance were so very kind to me. They attached a rope to the restroom door that I could pull in order to open it and pull myself inside. This was before anyone even thought of the automatic push-button doors. They often gave me soups with easy-open pop-top lids to take home. Sometimes they would send me home with baskets of food and other items. I have always appreciated their kindness, but, above all, Connie was a true friend, an angel who gave of herself, which is the truest gift of all.

❖

I didn't see Betty again until Christmas, when I went to a Christmas party at the Recreation Center for the Physically Limited, which is almost next door, behind Murdock Villa. At first I wasn't sure it was Betty. I could only see her back, but when she turned around, I was filled with that same feeling for her all over again.

I asked her how she was; she said, "Fine." It was a little awkward, like we were getting to know each other all over again.

One day that winter, after the New Year, I became very restless sitting in my apartment. I decided to go and visit Betty. I knew I should call her first on the TTY; I tried several times, but there was no answer. I knew she was home and that she liked to sleep late, so I thought I'd go over anyway, and maybe I'd get there just as she woke up. I hoped she would not be angry with me for making the trip in the snow.

I bundled up and started out on the four miles to her house. It was thirty-five degrees outside, and the snow had only melted away in patches. I tried to stay on the clear areas, but it was a difficult trip. My arms became hard to move because they were so cold, and the control lever on my chair was sticking because the frigid air had frozen the mechanism. Sometimes it would stick in one spot, and the chair would not stop when it was supposed to.

When I arrived at her place, I realized that I could not go up the steps and ring the doorbell. It seemed like forever before some people came by to whom I could write a note asking them to please ring the doorbell. Betty appeared at the door, surprised but happy to see me. She hurried inside and grabbed the old wooden door that we kept for getting my wheelchair up the steps. She got behind my chair and helped push me into the apartment. She quickly began wiping ice and moisture off the wheelchair and helped me warm up by giving me some hot tea.

I told Betty that my father and stepmother were supposed to come for a visit that afternoon. As it turned out, they came by Betty's and were surprised to find me there. They stayed and chatted for about two hours with the help of signs, gestures, and pictures, and we understood each other fairly well. They told me news about my sister in Washington State, my brother in California, and another sister who was traveling the world with her husband in a small boat. Paul Howard, I already knew, was working as a dental assistant in Oklahoma City.

After my parents left and as it neared ten o'clock, I decided I should leave. Betty said she wanted to go with me because it was so dark and cold. Before my father left, he had remarked that the temperature was supposed to drop to zero that night. Betty put on her heavy jumpsuit, and I put on gloves and a winter mask so that just my eyes, nose, and mouth showed. When we left the building, the chill in the air surprised me and I noticed that it was much colder than it was earlier.

Betty was on her bicycle, and I was following her, but then she slowed down and came to a stop. I wondered what she was doing. When I caught up with her, she pointed to a sprig of mistletoe hanging from a tree. She climbed onto my lap and gave me a kiss. Then she told me that she loved me, and I told her that I felt the same for her. Even though it was freezing cold, we both felt the warm glow of love.

As we continued on, the cold air began affecting the part of my arm that is paralyzed, and I could not push the controls on my chair properly. I could not keep the chair on a straight path but kept veering to the right. I asked Betty if we could try having her push the controls for me.

She signed, "What about my bike?"

I suggested that we try it with her and the bike on my lap, and that is what we did. It was awkward, and passersby must have thought we were a weird pair, but it worked well enough.

In fact, some people stopped and asked if they could help, but we told them, "No, thank you. We're fine."

In downtown Tulsa, a sudden burst of strong wind blew my cowboy hat off. Betty ran to get it, and luckily there were few cars on the street. By now we had come to a large empty parking lot, which I decided to cross. Another blast of wind came and blew my orange windbreaker up in my face so that I couldn't see where I was going. As Betty returned with my hat, she laughed as she watched my wheelchair turn round and round in circles in the parking lot. When we were almost home, we stopped again to look at the beautiful stars. It was a clear night and, indeed, a beautiful sight. We held each other, looked at the stars, kissed, and went on home. We sipped hot tea to warm ourselves from our excursion, and Betty left on her bicycle to go back to her place. I waited a little while, then called her on the TTY to make sure she arrived home safely.

# 12

## The Van

The next most significant development in my efforts to acquire independence occurred in summer 1982, when I got my specially equipped van. With the van, I could drive myself around town in all kinds of weather without having to rely on the wheelchair. More importantly, I had a more convenient means of travel to and from work.

A man named Pat Eidchun, who was on the Oklahoma Rehabilitation Council and involved with the Lion's Club, helped raise money to buy a van for me. I looked around and chose the one that I wanted—a 1978 Chevrolet. Of course, when I first got the van, it did not have the wheelchair lift, driving aids, and related equipment that I needed to operate it, so it sat in the parking lot for a long time waiting for the special equipment to be installed.

Eventually I was able to start practicing to drive the van. Driving a van was not a completely new experience for me. I had taken driver's training at the center, practicing with a van that belonged to the school, and I got a driver's license in Virginia. But I discovered that it was necessary to take another test in order to receive an Oklahoma driver's license. So I began learning to drive this van. I drove it around Murdock Villa and in the parking lot of a nearby church. One of the interpreters from TSHA helped me practice driving and helped me get my license. It was pretty scary when I drove the van alone for the first time. Stopping at stop signs was the scariest part, and it took a few months to get really good at it.

In summer 1983, I had a wreck in the van. I was feeling pretty happy that afternoon because it was the start of my two-week vaca-

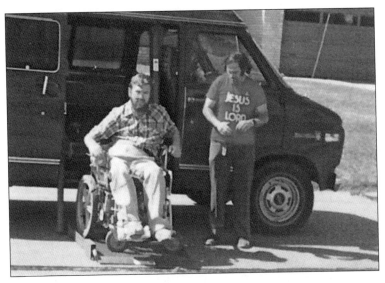

Don and his specially equipped van.

tion. I went to pick up Betty from her job, but I was about fifteen minutes early and had to wait for her. She saw me through the window, grinned, waved, and gave me the sign for "I love you." At four o'clock, she appeared and, with a happy smile, jumped into the van.

I asked her if she wanted to go straight home, and she said, "Yes."

I stayed about thirty minutes at her place—she still lived at the Denver Avenue address—and then said goodbye and left. I had forgotten about the heavy five o'clock traffic. It was very bad on the expressway. My brakes also were not working too well. A lady in a small car in front of me was repeatedly putting on her brakes and going very slowly. I wanted to pass her, but I could never seem to get around her because the car in the other lane kept blocking me. I edged up very close behind her, trying to get around, and before I knew it the whole right side of the van was crumpled against the concrete barrier wall. The only thing I remember feeling before passing out was the sensation of flying.

When I came to, I felt something dripping down the inside of my arm. I opened my eyes and saw red, and I knew it was blood.

My head was down near the floorboard, and I realized that I was in the passenger seat instead of the driver's seat. I focused my eyes to one side and saw my own ear, just dangling there. I was becoming soaked with blood, and I could see blood on the floorboard.

When I tried to push my body to an upright position, my arm was thrown outside the window, which made things even more awkward. When I managed to pull my arm back inside and get myself situated, I looked out at the cars going by, and no one had stopped.

I silently thanked the Lord that I was alive and was glad that neither Betty nor Jimmy, who lived with me and was my care provider at the time, was with me. I wondered how long it would be before someone came. About five minutes later, a semitrailer with a long tank stopped, and a man got out and came to the van. I saw his lips move, but I told him with a gesture that I could not hear. He understood and motioned that he would call for help. He went back to his truck and radioed for help.

The next thing I knew, a beautiful lady was there, saying something to me, and I had to tell her that I could not hear. She tried very hard to make herself understood. She spoke slowly and distinctly and was easy to lip-read, and her facial expressions made her messages clear.

She asked, "Can you feel anything?"

I motioned to her that I could from the chest up. She asked me which hospital I wanted to go to. From my position in the van, I could see her talking to the policeman when he arrived, but I never did talk to the policeman. The lady waited with me until the ambulance came, and then she left.

The paramedic tried to open the door on the driver's side of the van but it was locked, and the door on my side was jammed up against the retaining wall. Through the little wing window, he was able to reach in and unlock the door. He tried to talk with me, and I let him know that I was deaf. He began prodding to see if anything was broken and asked me if anything was injured other than my ear. I told him no, which turned out to be correct, but my ear was almost completely severed from my head. He put foam around my neck to protect it as the paramedics moved me out of the van onto a stretcher and into the ambulance.

In the hospital emergency room, I waited a long time on a table until the doctor came. The doctor gestured in order to ask if I could move my neck. I let him know that I could, and he removed the foam so a plastic surgeon could come and take care of my ear. The plastic surgeon and a nurse could not find a vein from which to take a blood sample but a second nurse was able to take the sample. She then asked me if I had family or someone I wanted to notify. I said no. So she inserted another needle and gave me something to make me sleep so the plastic surgeon could do the surgery.

When I woke up, it was three o'clock the next morning. I was glad that my family didn't know where I was. I didn't want them to worry or to have to come all the way from Oklahoma City. I decided to call TSHA to get an interpreter because I figured the doctor and nurses would have a lot of questions for me. I also thought the policeman, who had come to the emergency room the night before, might come back to ask me questions. A nurse made the call for me, talked to the interpreter coordinator, and found out that Betty had called TSHA several times asking if they had heard from me. Shortly thereafter, Debbie Ravenscroft, an interpreter who had interpreted for me many times before, arrived, and the doctor came in to check my ear.

When Betty arrived, she took charge, asking questions and wanting to know everything. I just lay there quietly, a little amused and, yet, touched by her caring. But I was concerned about my van. In the emergency room the night before, I had asked the policeman, who was there, and who had not appeared to be very patient, about the van. He had said he would let me know. Now that the surgery was over and I was awake, I was ready to know what had happened to it.

Through the interpreter, I asked the nurse about the van, and she had a note from the policeman about where I could find it.

Betty and Debbie went to pick it up. There was, of course, much damage to the van and it had to go to the shop for repairs. It already had several problems, including the brakes, which needed repair even before the accident. But now I found that my electric wheelchair had also been damaged in the accident, and it too had to go to the shop for repair. The frame had been badly bent, and another one had to be ordered. In the meantime, I had to use the old-model, nonelectric wheelchair that I had at home. I was only in the hospital for two days, but the other repairs took a matter of weeks.

Before I got either the electric wheelchair or the van back, vacation was over and I had to return to work. It was back to the bus. Insurance took care of the repairs to the van, but it did not cover repairs to the wheelchair. I worried about where I would get the money to pay for it, but when I went to the shop to pick up the wheelchair, I found that some mysterious lady had already paid for it. I never found out who she was. I was so thankful.

# 13

## Wedding Day

Just before Christmas 1983, I gave Betty a friendship ring. We had called off our engagement, and although we still saw each other from time to time, it did not seem we would ever put things back together again. Betty planned to move back to Virginia in early spring. So the ring was to be a gift, something for her to remember me by.

I drove to Telex and waited in the van until it was time for her to leave work. When she came out the door, she was surprised to see me, but she hurried to the van and opened the door. In the seat where she normally sat, I had placed a small box.

"What is this?" she asked.

"Get in and see," I replied in sign.

She scrambled up into the passenger seat and held the box in her lap, anxiously shaking it at the same time.

I told her to go ahead and open it, and she replied, "But it's not Christmas yet."

"That's okay, it's a special gift," I said.

She opened the box and saw that it was full of those little white Styrofoam pieces that look like snow. She dug in and pulled out another box. Inside the smaller box she found a card, on which there was a Bible and the words: "God Bless You." Inside, I had written about my feelings for her, and she read carefully, intently. On the back of the card, she noticed the words: "Look in Don's pocket."

"I like this—it's fun," she signed as she reached her hand into my shirt pocket, and I laughed as she pulled out the little velvety box.

The box held a little gold ring that spelled out the word "LOVE" with a tiny diamond. Betty smiled and gave me a hug and a kiss. I explained to her how I felt and why I had given her the ring.

"You are the only one close to me in the whole world," I said. "God bless you for helping me so much."

She brushed a tear from her eye. I knew that she had accepted and understood.

Spring came, but Betty did not go to Virginia. One Sunday in March, I went to church. Betty was supposed to be there, but she did not come. It occurred to me that something might be wrong, so on my way to work the following Monday morning, I went around behind her apartment and waited in my van for the bus that she usually took to work. When the bus arrived, Betty was not there.

When Betty's neighbor, a deaf girl, came out to walk to the bus stop, I asked her to knock on Betty's door and let her know I was there. Betty was sleeping right near the door, and when she learned that I was there, she came running out and hugged me. I was relieved, and I kept asking her if she was all right. She hugged me, clung to me for a long time, and I had the feeling that something was wrong. Then she said she needed to use the telephone and went back in and everything seemed fine, so I went on to work.

One day a week later, she was very excited. She had decided that she did not want to move back to Virginia after all. Instead, she wanted to stay in Tulsa and marry me. She felt strongly that God had told her to stay with me and marry me. I was taken by surprise, but I was delighted by the prospect that we were to be married at last.

The next Sunday, we were sitting together in church, but she seemed strange. She looked tired, like she didn't feel well, and she kept watching me all the time. Later, she went into another room, and our friend, Joan Morton, called me in to talk to her. I hugged Betty and asked her what was wrong. Her arms were limp, and she had been crying. She said she wanted to talk about marriage now, but first, she needed to find out what was going on with her health.

A few members of the church were kind enough to drive Betty to the emergency room, and I followed in my van because she was too weak to get in with me. After some tests, the doctors found that an allergy had caused the glands in her throat to swell. At this time, she was living in a Central Assembly of God apartment, and her room was near the laundry room. Her allergic reaction was being caused by the fabric softener used in dryers to control static electricity. Somehow the fumes were being vented from the laundry room into her room. The doctors gave her an inhaler, and I dropped her off at her home.

After Betty and I discussed it, we decided that the best option was for Betty to temporarily go to Virginia because the nurse there knew Betty well and could find out what was causing all of her health problems. When she returned, she did not want to move back into her old apartment. Instead, she moved in with me at Murdock Villa in April. Even though we set the wedding for July 28, 1984, we decided to put on our wedding rings so we wouldn't lose them.

Betty had returned to work at Telex when she got back from Virginia, but she quit the second week of July in anticipation of our marriage. Because of the difficulties of rising early to take care of me, working eight hours, riding the bus for an hour to get home, and taking care of me in the evenings, on top of her health issues, we decided it would be best for Betty to stop working at Telex. While I was at work, she would have some time for herself to bicycle or see friends.

We scheduled the wedding for seven o'clock on a Saturday morning amid the tall trees of Tulsa's Woodward Park. I sent an invitation telling everyone to wear pajamas (they didn't), and our friends Martha and Wilbur (Ma and Pa) hosted a reception beforehand with a meal and a cake.

Betty trimmed my hair and rolled her hair with rags so it would come out with pretty little curls. I bought a baby blue suit and

Don and Betty's wedding.

learned to tie a tie with Paul Howard's help. Betty got her dress from an interpreter friend named Karie Ray, and Ma helped her put on her dress. The preacher was a man named LaVerle Carrington who had a deaf wife and could sign. Betty helped me dress because there was no one at the house at the time to help me. Betty's father put a penny in her shoe, and she had a beautiful lace Bible cover. Betty loved her flowers. My father and stepmother; sister, Kathy; brothers, Paul Howard and Kendall; and Kendall's ten-year-old daughter, Leah, were all there.

With family and friends assembled, Wilbur escorted Betty down an aisle of cool, green grass to stand beside me. She wore a long, white dress with lots of lace, and she carried a bouquet of white, yellow, and blue daisies—she looked very lovely. The ring bearer had one of those pillows with fake rings on it. Since we had forgotten to put the real rings on it, we panicked when the preacher went to get them during the ceremony, but he just used the fake rings.

My third dream was to get married, and it was coming true. We lit two candles, joined them together to light one candle, and I felt such joy. I had achieved independence and employment, and now I was getting married. I could hardly believe it.

We paid twenty-five dollars to use the park for an hour, so we had to hurry. Instead of wine, we had orange juice and coffee. Betty had said absolutely no alcohol; she had had a bad experience before with me when I had gotten drunk and behaved badly, so I promised we would have only juice. We crossed our arms to drink our juice like a fancy toast and almost spilled it all over each other.

Also, instead of a tiered wedding cake, we had a pyramid of doughnuts, decorated with white ribbons and little white bells fashioned from sugar and topped with a little couple—one in a wheelchair. Leave it to us to never do anything the conventional way.

I had so much fun pulling up Betty's dress to take off her garter belt—I actually was able to use my hands to do it, with a little help from my mouth—and I figured out how to flip it into the air, right into Billy Ingram's hands. Billy was a wild man and quite a flirt, so it was very funny. Kendall's daughter, Leah, caught Betty's flowers. Then we packed up, changed clothes, and went to a deaf revival at our church. We hurried because we were late, and we stayed there until very late that night.

I always chuckle when I look back on that day because my electric wheelchair didn't stop very well on hills. All during the wedding, my chair kept moving ever so slowly backwards, so the preacher and the entire wedding party had to keep edging forward. What a great day.

# 14

## Woody

Woody Osburn was born in 1951 in the Cherokee Indian Hospital in Tahlequah, Oklahoma. He was the fourth of five children, and he was a quarter Cherokee, from his paternal grandmother, who was a full-blood Cherokee. The Osburn family lived in Morris, only a few miles away from Tahlequah, until Woody was five. Then the family moved to Dickson, Oklahoma, just outside of Ardmore, so Woody's father could get vocational training at a tech school. His father made leather saddles and the designs on belts at a tool and dye factory that had twelve employees. Woody told me they lived in the country because it was cheaper, and those were the first really vivid memories of his life.

Woody also told me he would ride with his family in the car to take his sister Joan to the Oklahoma School for the Deaf in Sulphur, thirty miles away, and drop her off there for the school week. That family tradition began when Joan was four years old, before Woody was even born. He remembered she would always cry when they dropped her off and eventually his parents made the mutual decision that his father would quit his job and they would all move to Sulphur. They moved to a house that was a block and a half from campus.

Woody told me it was like a revolving door at his house, with Joan's deaf friends coming and going. He had another sister and two brothers and lots of friends. It was a really small house, and it was always full of kids, deaf and hearing. Woody learned signs, but he always told me he felt he did not learn to sign as well as he should have, but he learned enough to get by. Joan was four years older than Woody, and she always had her friends around. He was the annoying little brother, and she was always running him off. He said he supposed part of his rebellion against her was that he didn't communicate well with her on purpose. But as he got older and tried harder, he got better at it. However, he would not say he was ever fluent in sign language.

I was older than Woody by nine or ten years, and I sometimes went to his house to visit Joan. This was how Woody and I first came to know each other. Years later, we ran into each other at Murdock Villa, where I lived. He lived on the sixth floor and I lived on the fifth floor, in apartment 523. We would pass one another in the hallway, and we would smile. He looked familiar, but the Woody I knew was a mobile person. We had a crude way of communicating, but I could read lips pretty well if the environment was just right.

One day, I stopped Woody and asked him if he was Joan's brother. Another time, Woody and his mother entered Murdock as I was going out, and she recognized me. She and I had a long conversation, and she served as my interpreter with Woody. Most of the time I saw Woody, he was behind the building—he was always outside reading, and I was usually there reading my Bible—and we struck up a casual friendship.

We got to know each other in part because we both went to Tulsa Independent Living Center, now called Ability Resources, for their services. This center focused on helping individuals with disabilities maintain their personal independence. It was a valuable resource located next to Murdock Villa.

It was on one of those days outside behind the building that Woody told me his story. Woody had lived in Chicago, where he worked at a bank for three years, and he had married a girl from the city. She wanted to move to Dallas, so they moved and Woody found a job at a bank there. However, they divorced after just a year of marriage, and after working in the bank all day, going home at night to sit by himself was the last thing Woody wanted to do.

LIFT complaints                    Tribune photo by Chris Horn 8/30/89
Roland Sykes, left, Woody Osburn and others listen to fellow LIFT users complain to Metropolitan Tulsa Transit Authority Tuesday about transportation for the disabled. Some protesters asked that a contract with MY Cab Co., LIFT operator, be rescinded. Story page 8A.

Roland and Woody. Photo by Chris Horn for the *Tulsa Tribune*. Used by permission.

To fill the lonely hours, Woody decided to get a second job. He went to a bartending academy for two weeks and learned how to mix drinks. He got a job at a restaurant/bar called "Old House," which is what it was, a big, old, colonial-style house. He worked there until two o'clock in the morning. He would leave the bank at four thirty in the afternoon, and he would change his clothes when he got to the restaurant at five o'clock.

On Thanksgiving Day in 1979, on Woody's way home from the bar, the long hours took their toll and he fell asleep at the wheel and rolled his car. This accident initially paralyzed him from the neck down, but with rehabilitation he regained some use of his arms over a year's time.

That is kind of how fate works. Woody had sold his car in Chicago because he didn't need one for the three years he lived there, but when he moved to Dallas, he saved up all of his money to buy a car. Then, at the age of twenty-eight, his life changed forever.

After he broke his neck, Woody spent six weeks in intensive care at Baylor Medical Center. The facility had eight beds; most of the people there were in comas, and several people died while he was there. He was in traction, the old-fashioned type where they put screws in the sides of his head, with twenty-five pounds of weight on his neck so that it would stay stable, much like what I experienced. It was a really bad time in his life.

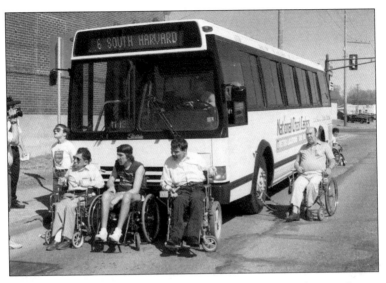

MTTA bus protest. Woody Osburn is on the right. Photo by Rabbit Hare for *Tulsa World*. Used by permission.

After six weeks of staring at the ceiling there, he rented a small Cessna plane with a paramedic and flew up to Tulsa. The doctors tried to talk him out of leaving, but he insisted. He did not want to stay at Baylor even though they said they had a "cutting-edge" rehab center. The Tulsa Rehabilitation Center at Hillcrest Hospital had fifty beds and a much better reputation. Moreover, his family wanted him with them. Woody was in Tulsa almost a year, after which he moved in with his mother for seven or eight months. Then he got an apartment at Murdock Villa, where he met me for the second time in his life. He moved into a two-bedroom apartment so he could have live-in aides. He had some who stole from him, and one who actually kept him captive in his own apartment for three days.

After I wrecked my van, Woody got a call from someone at Vocational Rehabilitation who asked him if his worker could drive me to and from work. The aide got paid well through a Medicaid program that subsidized her income, and VR reimbursed Woody for the mileage on his van. The aide took me to work for a couple of months, and she helped me with other things as well, and I was glad for the help.

Roland Sykes had been named as the new director of the Tulsa Independent Living Center. The center provided information and referrals, skills training (independent living), peer support, advocacy—all new services since Roland started and got the center involved in accessibility in general. The biggest problem Woody and I had found was that it was very difficult to find people to work for you and reliable programs that were trustworthy. Woody paid his first attendants out of his pocket, for the most part; he got some help, but not enough. That was why he had moved in with his mother at first. It was the only option he had at the time, but no one wants to live with their mother at age twenty-nine. Murdock Villa was the only option for Woody and I for independent living. Recruiting and hiring aides has always been one of the biggest issues for quads. The programs that existed back then didn't pay enough money; even now, they still don't.

In the 1970s and 1980s, the Americans with Disabilities Act (ADA) was not on anyone's radar. There was a lack of transportation and affordable housing, which was why we lived in the projects. Both public and private buildings lacked accessibility, and no one was ready for disabled people to be mainstreamed into society, so everything we did was a challenge. Woody knew another resident at Murdock Villa who the police were constantly bringing home because he would go five miles in his wheelchair and get stuck in the road. The cops would pick him up and bring him back because they knew where he lived. He was just a very independent person. He had muscular dystrophy, and he used to push his big chair with his feet and roll backwards. But one day, he was crossing Utica Avenue on his way to his bank, and an older lady squashed him with her car. He was absolutely flattened; the accident knocked him out of his chair and broke his arms and legs. The bank started a fund for him, and they bought him a new motorized chair, made in England. The chair he had was an old Emerson

Jennings, and they all looked alike, so he bought a new one that could jump curbs. We all had to become creative so we could get around.

One day, when Woody was in rehab, he had a fire lit under him. This would be a life-changer for everyone like us for years to come. The rehab center at Hillcrest had at least a dozen donated buses and vans, but it only used one to take people somewhere on Tuesday nights, usually to places like a Mexican restaurant or a movie theater. Everyone went as a group, and the rehab center would put a transportation schedule on the calendar and you had to sign up to go. About five nurses and a driver would go with the group.

At that time, there were some group sessions at the rehab center led by a psychologist, Ken Slade, who would meet with us and let us talk about our problems. We would vent, listen, share experiences, and blow off steam.

Once, Ken's girlfriend, Sharon, came in as a guest speaker and told us about government services we had not known about. She told us about a commission from Oklahoma City, appointed by the governor, which oversaw the hospitals in Oklahoma. This commission had scheduled a public hearing downtown the next day, a Tuesday. Woody talked to Sharon afterward and said he wanted to go, but the problem was transportation.

Sharon commented, "Well, you have all those buses outside."

I could see the light come on in Woody's eyes and the wheels turning in his brain.

Then Woody sighed to himself and said, "This is just a matter of me asking."

And thus the whole thing began.

Woody asked at the nurses' station, and they kicked it downstairs to the director of the rehab center, a man named Doyle Knowles, who was about sixty years old and a paraplegic. Doyle had been an accountant at Hillcrest for about seventeen years before he was promoted to director of the rehab center, and his only qualification seemed to be that he was disabled. Woody made an appointment for three o'clock that afternoon, and he went down a narrow hallway to get to Doyle's little office.

There, Woody asked Doyle about using the bus to get to the public hearing. To Woody's surprise, Doyle asked him why he would want to go.

Woody tried to swallow his astonishment. "Education," he said. "It sounds like useful information."

"Well, people tend to go to these things, and they make a lot of trouble," Doyle said.

"Frankly I don't know what you are talking about," Woody said. "I am just asking you for one of twelve vehicles for one night to go to this thing."

After some back and forth came the straw that broke the camel's back.

Doyle looked right at Woody and said, "People like you remind me of the Negroes of the '60s."

Woody didn't say anything for a moment but made a mental note of the man's name. He looked at this man in a three-piece suit in a wheelchair across from him and wondered what kind of a person would say such a thing.

Then Woody said, "We will see about this," and left the office.

Woody's doctor was also the director of the hospital, so Woody went to the nurses' station and asked to talk to his doctor. However, by the time Woody got back upstairs, everyone's antennae was already up; the speed at which information spread was worse than a small town. He didn't get anywhere with his request, so he kept talking about the hearing and the transportation issue. All this had happened within a matter of three hours, and Woody was getting really mad. After Woody finished his afternoon rehab an hour later, he was on his way back upstairs and met his recreational therapist coming down the hallway. She was carrying a clipboard and a pen.

"Woody, Doyle says if you get fourteen other signatures from people who are coming to this event, you can use the bus," she said.

Woody only had until 5 p.m., so he got the therapist to help him, pushing him in his chair down the hallway into people's rooms. He got twenty signatures. The therapist rushed him downstairs, and they triumphantly slammed the petition on Doyle's desk and got the bus. In fact, no one really wanted to go except one paraplegic guy who was ticked off enough to want to find out what this meeting was about and why the director didn't want us to go. We went with seven staff members in an ancient school bus to the old Tulsa convention center downtown. The meeting was up on the second level. When we arrived, we noticed that all of the people were dressed in their suits and we had our sweat suits on from rehab. We were all, as Woody would say, "gnarly-looking." Woody went up first because the elevators were really crowded. We had to stop and sign in. The lady took our names and wrote them for us.

It was auditorium-style seating, so the only place for us to sit in our wheelchairs was at the front of the room. The room had bright red carpeting and large wooden pillars. Woody immediately noticed Doyle Knowles sitting next to one of those wooden pillars, and a mischievous smile came across his face.

"Let's go sit with Doyle," he said.

Woody had a manual chair with "quad knobs" on it to push, and it took forever to get down to where Doyle sat. We pulled up as close as we could to Doyle so he couldn't operate his chair. Woody parked right next to him, trapping him in. Doyle had on a three-piece gray suit and a tie. I could just see his face filling up with blood until it was beet red. The chairman of the meeting was smoking a cigar while he ran the meeting. All the people leading the meeting were "cigar-chomper-type guys," as Woody called them, in expensive suits, and they had oversight over us. There we were, looking like we were in our living rooms and like we hadn't been bathed in a week; our hair wasn't even combed.

The meeting started, and they made a presentation that was like muddled information to us because we were new to the game. They got to the question-and-answer part, and a lady began walking around with a microphone taking questions. Woody kept his hand up for what seemed like forever. After quite a long while, the woman came over to Woody, who told the commission everything that had happened so far.

"You know, I have been in rehab a long time," Woody said, "and I have taken the bus every Tuesday night to get ice cream, to get pancakes, to get Mexican food, to go to the movies, but the one time I needed it to come down here to listen to the people who are in charge of my life right now, the answer was, 'You remind me of the Negroes of the '60s.' That was the answer."

The room went silent. You could have heard a pin drop.

"Do you know who the section 504 coordinator of Hillcrest hospital is?" Woody asked, as Sharon had told him to.

The chairman took his cigar out of his mouth and said, "Doyle, would you like to address that question?"

Doyle looked up slowly, took a breath, and mumbled, "I will take care of the section 504 coordinator."

"You will take care of him, how?" Woody asked, "By paying him off?"

"You can't talk to me that way," Doyle countered.

"I can certainly talk to you any way I want. I am a grown man," Woody calmly replied.

Woody had already told the commission how much money they were getting from us every month, which was thousands of dollars. Rehab cost about a dollar a minute, for two hours at a time in the morning and in the afternoon, and our beds were about $500 a day. Woody had a $250,000 insurance policy from his job in Dallas that had run out in no time, so he was not a person to argue with.

That day, a fire was lit under Woody that burned bright for years afterward and never went out. Woody and I could now clearly see who the good guys were and who the bad guys were and who would not risk anything. These people did not want to teach us how to live in the community. All they wanted was to "do rehab on us." We did all the work. They were not preparing us for independence in the community or for the workforce. There was no transportation, no affordable housing, and no accessibility whatsoever. Caregiving was the main issue. If you didn't have a place to live with a reliable caregiver, you could end up in an institution or living with your mother.

In 1986, the City of Tulsa's Private Industry Training Council and the Warren Foundation were working with a man named Dr. Perry Sanders, who, even though he is blind, could see further into the future than anyone I knew. Maurice Morrison, who was working with transportation for the disabled, asked Dr. Sanders to head a committee on transportation services for the blind and disabled, and he accepted. It was an election year, and the candidates for mayor were Dick Crawford, a Republican; Tom Quinn, who ran as an independent; and Terry Young, the Democratic incumbent running for reelection.

Dr. Sanders asked all the candidates to appear at a committee meeting at New View Services, a local community volunteer agency, and address their needs. Crawford was the only one who came. He was not expected to gain enough votes to become mayor, but he listened to the complaints of the disabled and said he would help if elected. Surprisingly, he won and became mayor of Tulsa. Crawford remained true to his word and set up a program that began to change things in Tulsa and that became a model for other cities. The disabled community was delighted. The changes were based on how blind people and those who used walkers, wheelchairs, and other adaptations would get around town more easily and be able to use the public transportation system.

However, the city buses were still not accessible, and the city did not have other vehicles accessible for wheelchair users. At the time, White Cab Company had a contract that stipulated they would pick up blind people or people who used walkers and take them where they needed to go, but those of us who used wheelchairs were frustrated. We could not go to doctor's appointments or go places when we needed to, just like other people. We felt like lesser people and like our needs were not being heard.

People were starting to protest in other states, such as Colorado, and the unrest was starting to be felt in Tulsa. By 1988, we decided that action must be taken, and I felt I should help fight, along with my friends Woody Osburn and Roland Sykes. They felt strongly that we must protest, as others were doing in other states. I was willing to chain myself to the buses if that was what it took to get attention, and that is exactly what I and many other disabled citizens in the community ended up doing.

We formed a group to address the transportation issue. We called it ADAPT—Americans for Disabled Accessible Public Transportation. Society wasn't adapting to us—we wanted to be in our own homes and have our own transportation, just like everyone else. Not only were the buses not providing lift equipment for those of us who needed it, but the Metropolitan Tulsa Transit Authority (MTTA) decided to increase the fare for disabled riders

Transportation protest. Photograph by Ron Hart for the *Tulsa World*. Used by permission.

to twice the fare nondisabled riders paid. We felt it was not only unfair, it was discriminatory, and the public took notice after we shut down traffic for more than an hour. After three protests in 1988, seven disabled individuals were arrested and fined, but we felt we had a worthy cause.

As a result of the protests, the city made capital funds available to purchase vans for the disabled community, and fixed route buses with wheelchair lifts were gradually integrated into the system. We got lifts on all the buses in Tulsa by 1989, one year before it was mandated nationwide. MTTA also reversed its decision to raise fares for disabled riders. I felt empowered after that—I stood up for what I believed in, and we prevailed.

After that, Woody and I tackled the nursing home issue. Our mission was to close down nursing homes and redirect that money into the community. During the Clinton administration, it became mandatory that a social worker had to inform you of your rights before the state could put you in a nursing home. You had the right to choose to live in the community, in a place of your choice, and the state would pay for your attendant. However, because there was never any oversight, no one ever told people of this option. They just signed you up and slid you into the nursing home. Some states offered programs that were not adequate, while other states refused to offer the option altogether.

All night vigil. Photograph by Gary Kruse for the *Tulsa Tribune*. Used by permission.

# 15

## The Zoo

Betty and I settled into our life at Murdock Villa and made friends. Betty had been saving for a Volkswagen but instead spent the money on a waterbed. She knew I would sleep better, and it would keep me from getting bedsores. It was great for me, but she began to get her days and nights mixed up because she was sleeping during the day while I was at work. Eventually, she moved to a sofa and then to a twin bed.

I had a light that I would pull at night if I needed anything. I made it myself. I had a trapeze bar over my bed with a chain that I could pull, and I could also use the bar to pull myself up. I love plants, and I liked to hang them on the trapeze and watch them grow. The judge who gave us our marriage license gave us a beautiful jade stone in the shape of a fish. I decided to also hang that on my trapeze where I could always see it.

It was August 1993. Betty and I heard about an event at the Tulsa Zoo called "Roar and Snore" that sounded like fun. The evening would consist of dinner, a movie, a train ride, animal demonstrations, and a campfire/campout. The following morning, breakfast would be provided. We were excited to attend, so we scheduled the lift bus and arrived at the zoo, anxious for the evening and morning with the animals.

That evening, the organizers assembled the participants under an American Airlines tent and set up a small TV screen and started the movie. Betty and I squinted at the mouths moving on the screen, but without the benefit of closed captions, we could not understand a word they were saying. After several minutes of

Don and Betty at the zoo.

this, it became quite tedious and we gave up trying to figure out what the movie was about. Our attention shifted to outside the tent. We looked at each other and immediately knew we needed to find something else to do. We slowly made our way out of the semi-darkened tent and into the fresh air of the zoo. We grinned with excitement and began to roam. We had no idea we were not supposed to leave the tent.

We traveled from exhibit to exhibit, Betty pointing and jumping when she saw an animal that amazed her. I loved to watch her as much as I loved watching the animals. The giraffes were our favorites. It was incredible to see them up close and to be able to touch them. Betty also particularly enjoyed a massive tortoise named Big Al.

Betty faced a difficult challenge when it was time to empty my urine bag. She felt bad because she was afraid to go into the men's restroom with me to empty it because she genuinely thought she would be arrested. In her mind, her only choice was to dump the urine in a flower bed. She even went to get water to cover up the smell, but she was relieved to find that the ground had absorbed it. She told me that God had made the smell disappear.

About that time, the zoo workers realized we were gone, began to panic, and caught up with us. We received a mild scolding for leaving the group, but they were relieved that we were okay. Betty explained to them that we could not understand the movie, and they understood. We went back for a wonderful dinner of hamburgers, and we roasted marshmallows and made s'mores. The zoo workers also gave us glow-in-the-dark cups.

We decided to bunk down for the night, Betty on a bench and me in my chair. We did not have any blankets because it was so hot, and we decided to "rough it" near the giraffe area. As the night went on, Betty contracted a sore throat. She told me the next morning that every time a painful swallow jarred her awake, she would stare into the eyes of a watchful giraffe nearby and it would calm her back to sleep.

# 16

## The Search

I was always looking for a way to fulfill my caretaking needs without the burden constantly falling on Betty. I needed to stay as healthy and independent as possible, but it was a constant struggle. I became more and more frustrated as the days, weeks, and months passed. Something had to change.

I was still working at Lowrance Electronics. I could no longer maintain the second van I had gotten after I wrecked the first one, so I relied on the lift bus for transportation. Betty had quit her job to help care for my needs, and at first we were both very happy. However, I began to notice that Betty was becoming a little unhappy when I wanted to get close to her. I wondered what the problem was, and I began to become impatient with her constant excuses to escape intimacy. These things were not easy for either of us, so we were both frustrated. As the days went on and Betty felt more pressure to take care of me, I began losing my temper when I felt my needs as a husband were being ignored. We started arguing a lot, and I said things to her that hurt her feelings.

Getting me in and out of bed and dressed, washing me, getting food and medicine, taking care of my bedsores and toileting needs, and dealing with my muscle spasms and other health issues was getting to be too much for Betty, and there were just not enough home care resources available. I knew I had to find a place to go live that offered these services on a twenty-four-hour basis. At times, people had to bring me food, and there were times I had to rely on volunteers to come care for me, if I had any care at all. Sometimes I could not even get myself to work. I would go to the Independent

Living Center for support and speak with my counselor in order to find out what I could do about my situation, and he would tell me that the only thing I could do was to quit my job.

I decided I had to go to Parkland Manor in Prague, Oklahoma. I heard it would be a good place with good care for me. I had also heard that the administrator there knew sign language. The process took some time, but I was accepted and moved there in 1995. I had been at Lowrance for thirteen years, but it was time to say goodbye.

Betty had decided to go to Virginia to be with her family. Her father had written to say he had come home and wanted to reunite the family. Betty thought this would be a good time to go home and try again to make peace with them, as well as take a break from us. Her health was waning, and she needed to clear her head and get in touch with her roots. A trip home would be good, she told me. Even though I would miss her deeply, I knew she needed to go. She had been away from her family for a while and it was time for her to go, and I felt I needed to move on myself.

I had to reduce my hours at Lowrance because, according to the state, if I worked too many hours, the state would not pay for my caregiver. By this time, I had already had to let my caregiver, Jewel, go. My brother Paul Howard had been living with me and doing his best to take care of me while Betty was gone. I felt it was time for a new beginning.

I quit Lowrance and moved to Parkland Manor. For me, giving up working, which had always been one of my dreams in life, was almost like giving up breathing. I felt like I was no longer a whole person. But I knew I had no choice. I had to find a place where I could get proper care and try to be as happy as I could. I never wanted to give up hope. I missed Betty terribly, and every letter that she wrote kept me going. When I arrived in Prague, I wrote letters to Betty, my family, and my friends.

# 17

## To Be Free

Woody graduated college in 1992, and Roland Sykes told the Tri-County Patriots For Independent Living (TRIPIL) organization about him because he thought Woody would be a perfect fit. Woody moved to Washington, Pennsylvania, to take a job as disability activist at TRIPIL, where he worked for Kathleen Kleinmann, the executive director.

He returned to Oklahoma in 1996 to visit his parents, who were divorced but lived across the street from each other in Sallisaw. One day, Woody went over to his mom's for breakfast. She asked if he had heard about me and the fact that I was living in a nursing home in Prague. Last Woody knew, I had transportation because I had obtained the second van. He also knew I had worked for a long time at Lowrance, because he had come to say goodbye before he went to Pennsylvania.

Woody knew that a nursing home in Prague was the last place I wanted to be, so something must be terribly wrong.

He called the Independent Living Center and asked, "Why is Don Fulk in a nursing home? How could you let this happen?"

My VR assistance, which paid for my attendants, was tied to my working, which I did not know when I quit my job. After I quit, I received a notice in the mail that my assistance was cut off for my attendant services. Then my second van fell apart. Woody said the whole thing sounded like a bad country-western song. He was very upset when he found out I was in a nursing home, but I had to go there or have no care and starve to death.

Woody immediately sprang into action. He had a driver, and before he knew it, he was planning a road trip to Prague. Once again, he asked his mother to serve as interpreter, since she had pretty good signing skills. When they arrived in Prague, Woody had the driver turn into a neighborhood.

He told the driver, "Come with me and we will walk. I don't want anyone to see my van."

It was a steamy Oklahoma July day, and Woody said he could see people inside the doorway of the nursing home smoking. Woody told me he walked up and pulled on the door, and it was locked. The workers inside motioned for them to go around, so they went around to the front.

There was a guy who said, "May I help you?"

"No," Woody replied, and he wheeled himself in to the front desk. "Is Don Fulk here?"

At first the woman didn't even look up.

Woody again said, "Excuse me."

I guess the woman thought Woody was just another wheelchair resident.

Then she looked up and he said again, "Is Don Fulk here?"

"Down that hallway to the right," she told him.

Down the hallway, Woody and his mother heard a lot of loud country music coming out of a room. A woman was mopping in the hallway, and nurses were down there smoking. Woody and his mother noticed all of the outside doors were locked, which was a violation of the fire code. They came into my room, and there was an old man in a bed, stretched out on his back with his mouth wide open. He seemed to be in a coma. A large floor TV boomed with a country music video station; it was cranked up as loud as it could go. Next to the comatose old man, the curtain was closed and the other half of the room was dark.

Woody's mother leaned down and turned the TV off. The music went silent. Woody wheeled over to the other side of the room and looked. I had my bed turned to where I was staring at a blank wall. I had a chest of drawers and a large computer that looked new, and my clothes hung in the closet. Woody turned his chair around and looked at me. I was sleeping, but I felt someone was there and opened my eyes. When I saw that it was Woody, I thought I must be dreaming.

"Are you an angel?" I signed.

"Hardly!" Woody said with a big grin.

Woody's mother came in and started interpreting. I couldn't believe my eyes. I could not hold back my joy and excitement to see my friend.

A worker came in and said, "Hey, who turned off the music?"

"I did," Woody's mother said. "Get out!"

I thought that was pretty funny. Woody then asked me what happened; I explained how I had ended up there and that the care wasn't good—no one knew how to take care of quadriplegics. I kept asking if he was an angel. I think I was depressed.

Woody said he had already thought about it on the way to Prague, and he asked me if I wanted to live here. I said no. He had taken a job in Harrisburg after working in Washington, Pennsylvania, and he knew Kathleen, at TRIPIL, would help me. Option number one, he told me, was a lawyer he knew named Stephen Gold who could help me. Before he could get the words out of his mouth, I was already telling him no.

"Wait, hear me out," he said.

"How long?" I asked, and Woody said, "One or two years."

"No way," I said. "What is your other option?"

"Well," he replied, "I am going back to Pennsylvania on Sunday. I can give you a ride."

It was a Thursday. I began nodding my head vigorously. Woody told me I couldn't act like that because the nursing home workers would sense something was up. So I calmed down. I began to feel hope and excitement welling up inside me for the first time in a long time.

"I parked my van out of sight," Woody continued.

"Sunday is perfect because I always go to the park and read my Bible," I told him.

"Okay," Woody said. "Where do we meet in the park?"

"By the swings, where the kids play," I said.

Woody replied, "I will be there at two o'clock, but don't panic if I am late. And remember, you can't do this. You gotta play your role and act normally. Go down and read your Bible, and I will pick you up and we will go. Don't tell anyone!"

The only person who could give permission for me to leave was my guardian, my brother, Paul Howard, and we both assumed he would say no, which was why we could not tell anyone.

Woody went to the desk because I was sweating like crazy. I had three nasty pressure sores, and he asked the nurse what she was doing for them.

"The usual," she said.

"What is the usual?"

"Saline solution," she said.

Woody was incensed. He told her that was equivalent to spitting on the sores and that the nurses needed to take care of them properly. His mother got a giant trash bag and filled it with medical supplies, clothing, and other things we would need. Woody told me that I would have to leave everything behind—my television, my furniture, and my computer. I told him I didn't care.

The trip to Pennsylvania would take around nineteen hours, and Woody wanted to go the scenic route, I-40 through Sallisaw to the Arkansas border, where I would no longer be a ward of the state of Oklahoma. Things didn't exactly happen that way. Woody had called a lawyer in Philadelphia, who asked him if he was really going through with his plan.

"What would be the worst that could happen if we got caught?" Woody asked him.

"Well," the lawyer replied. "Police maybe will pick you up and charge you with warrants and kidnapping and take him back, but it will probably not stick."

So we had this in the back of our minds the whole time.

Woody and his driver, Kenny, arrived at the park a couple of hours late, but the important thing was that they got there. Woody was a smoker then and the air conditioning was not working in the van, so Woody sat outside and smoked and looked for me. It was a quiet Sunday afternoon and the only person Woody and Kenny could see was someone across the street patching his roof. The air was still, and they could feel the tension. They drove around the park to see if they could find me. As they drove, all of a sudden they saw me flash by about two blocks away.

"I saw him," Woody said. "He will be here in a minute. Just go back to the swing set."

They had a couple more cigarettes. I still didn't show, so they drove the same route again. All of a sudden, there I was right in front of them, motoring in my wheelchair along the shoulder of the road. Woody saw a police officer stop and try to talk to me. He also saw a police car that appeared to follow me, and a nurse outside talking with an officer, so Woody and Kenny were becoming paranoid at that point. When they saw me, Kenny started honking the horn.

"Kenny, he's deaf!" Woody said.

Kenny had warrants on him and an illegal driver's license. He was freaking out; he did not want to do this, period. They pulled up next to me, and they were making crazy hand motions and pointing, then they drove away so I tried to go meet them. They went to the swings and I wasn't there.

"For crying out loud," Woody yelled. "Go to the church!"

I had ended up over at the church because I thought I was being followed by a cop. When I pulled in to the church, I noticed that the parking lot was gravel and my wheelchair was struggling for traction. Woody was watching the police officer talk to the nurse, and I backed into Kenny's vehicle, my wheels spinning.

Kenny was yelling at me, and Woody was yelling at Kenny, "He is still deaf!"

Finally Woody lost it and said, "Both of you guys look at me! Calm down. Calm down! Drive to the left and wait!" We all collectively sighed and tried to, as Woody would say, "chill out."

Kenny helped me onto the lift and got me into the van. He was about to, as he said, "haul ass," but Woody told him to drive fifteen miles an hour and not attract attention. It was hard because Kenny was vibrating, he was so nervous. He slowly drove to Main Street because Interstate 40 was seven miles away, and there we were, in the middle of Main Street on a Sunday afternoon and the only car we passed was, of course, that police officer. When I saw the officer, I started praying and rocking back and forth.

"For crying out loud," Woody said again.

We got to I-40, and that's where Woody said he blew it, because if he had known about the other route, we would have been out of Oklahoma in less an hour. Instead, we went on the turnpike to Tulsa. It was so hot that day with no air conditioning in Woody's van. Woody was dying of thirst, and he needed something cold to drink. As a quad, when your body overheats, you need something cold, and you need it right away.

"Stop at McDonald's," Woody said, but Kenny would not stop because he was so nervous.

"Kenny, if you value your job, you will stop."

So we stopped at a convenience store, and we got a bag of ice, cups, and drinks.

Woody told us again to calm down because we kept saying, "Let's go, let's go!"

We came to the Joplin exit and, for some reason, we ended up in downtown Tulsa. I pointed out where I used to live and where I used to work, at Lowrance Electronics. It was as though we were doing a victory lap of Tulsa one last time.

We got to the state line at dusk. It had taken three and half hours, which seemed like forever, just to get out of Oklahoma. We paid the toll and crossed over into Missouri.

"Don, you are free," Woody said to me, and I started praying again.

We drove until 10 p.m., when Woody told Kenny to take the next exit so we could eat. Kenny said no and they argued again, but we finally stopped. I refused to get out, so we compromised and Kenny brought out three chicken fried steaks and we ate in the van.

When we finished eating, Woody thought he should call the nursing home and let them know I was okay so my family would not worry. I had a long argument with him because in order to let him out of the van, I had to get out.

Woody looked at me sternly and said, "Don, no one is looking for us in Missouri at eleven o'clock at night."

I let him out of the van and he got on a pay phone. He could hear activity because of the shift change at the nursing home.

Woody told them that he was a friend of Don Fulk and, after a pause, he said, "Please tell his family he is fine and he is going to live with a friend."

Then he hung up and became really paranoid.

"Get in the van, get in the van, get in the van!"

We drove all night and when we arrived at a giant travel plaza on the Ohio state line, Woody started hollering, "Please stop, I gotta get out of here! I gotta get some air!"

Woody had dual tanks on that van. Kenny knew we didn't need to stop for gas, but he knew we needed a break. He took off our shirts, gave us baths, brushed our hair, put clean shirts on us, and we felt human again. A lot of people didn't pay attention to us. We went up under an awning near the bathrooms.

Suddenly, a police officer walked straight toward us. I could see Woody and Kenny holding their breath.

He was a big guy, and he walked up slowly, staring down at us. "How you doing?" he asked, and then he nodded and walked off.

I looked at Woody and Kenny and smiled and said, "gotcha!"

Woody howled with laughter.

It was afternoon when we arrived in Washington, Pennsylvania, and pulled up into Kathleen Kleinmann's driveway. Roland Sykes was there too, anxiously waiting. Kathleen had arranged for a nurse and a medical equipment specialist to be at the house, and she had a hospital bed in her living room for me. It was quite an event. They did an evaluation on me right there.

"This man needs to be in the hospital," the nurse said.

"Let's see how he does overnight," Kathleen responded.

When I didn't do well, they took me to Alleghany General the next day while Woody drove on back to Harrisburg. Roland gave me $3,000 in cash. When I gave him a confused look, he said, "you may need it."

TRIPIL is an agency that, among other things, works with the disabled community providing peer support, information and referral, and transitioning from nursing homes or hospitals to independent living in the community. When Kathleen began as executive director in the early 1990s, these were brand new concepts and very few people knew how to make progress on these issues, especially in the area of transportation.

Kathleen sought the guidance of Roland Sykes, who was Executive Director of Ability Resources in Tulsa, Oklahoma, and who had made great strides in the transportation movement with Woody and me. We had lit a fire under MTTA, and Kathleen enlisted Roland's help to start her own fire in Pennsylvania. It was good to see Roland again.

I spent a year in Alleghany General Hospital. That year was not pleasant. The only times I felt comforted were the times I received calls or visits from my sweet Betty. At one point, they sent me to a hospital in West Virginia for surgery. Before it was over, I ended up having several surgeries and lots of antibiotics. Many times, the hospital threatened to kick me out because I had no money to pay, but Kathleen and her staff stood by me. We all stayed strong and said we would not leave until I got the proper treatment. At long last, Roxanne Huss, one of Kathleen's staff, found an article in a magazine about a special vacuum treatment for bedsores that was revolutionary but very expensive. The hospital was intrigued because it was new and different, and they agreed to try it. We couldn't believe that it worked.

At the hospital, I sometimes had an interpreter; a really nice red-headed guy in his thirties. Mostly I wrote notes on a clipboard with a felt pen in my mouth. The last time Woody and I visited, he came into my room and we talked for three hours. We talked about the old days back when we did the bus protest.

"Someday," I said, "Woody, you and I will be old men and need to retire. Let's plan to live with each other and retire together."

That was the last time I saw Woody.

Kathleen got me round-the-clock caregivers because my health was not good. When I got out of the hospital, I moved into an apartment two blocks from the TRIPIL office. I was starting to be able to sit in my wheelchair for short periods of time. I was looking forward to volunteering at TRIPIL and helping others like me.

I was so happy. I was free.

# EPILOGUE

Don was found on February 4, 1998, in his bed with his Bible, smiling and peacefully sleeping forever. He has touched lives, inspired so many disabled and abled people to appreciate what they have, to work hard, to achieve their dreams, and always do it with a kind heart and a sense of humor. Don's brothers and sisters are quoted as saying that everyone who had the pleasure of meeting Don was inspired by his smile and positive attitude and he made a difference wherever he went. He found a quiet purpose in his life.

When Don was four years old, one of the boys in his neighborhood burned his hand with a cigarette lighter. The scar gradually healed and faded away. As it turned out, that would be one of the least of the scars Don would bear during his life, but he bore all of them with amazing strength, a wonderful sense of humor, and warmth of spirit. I am proud to have known this man. He taught me so much about patience, love, and the ability to overcome even seemingly insurmountable odds.

Because of Don Fulk, Woody Osburn, and Roland Sykes, Oklahoma and Pennsylvania now have city bus lift services for the disabled community. TRIPIL, which started with a staff of fifteen, now has a staff of sixty, and Medicaid now pays to bring individuals out of nursing homes into independent living situations on a daily basis. TRIPIL is one of the only agencies that provides conferences that teach agencies how to "free" people like Don.

Looking back on those beautiful, sunny summer days I spent with him as we sat together in my yard, he in his great iron wheelchair and me in my shorts, cross-legged in the grass, I remember looking up at him, intensely watching his hands as they moved slowly, sometimes not so steadily, in the air with closed fists. I also remember squinting into the brightness, not wanting to miss a sign or an expression on his wonderful face, listening to those silent stories and marveling at the experiences and feelings he shared with me. I would stop him every so often to write furiously on my yellow notepad and repeat his signs back to him to make sure I understood everything and had gotten the story exactly right.

From time to time, he would lower his exhausted arms and blink a few times. This was his signal for water. Because he could not sweat normally, I knew what he needed me to do. I would run inside and come back out with a large cup full of ice-cold water and dump it on Don's head. He would shake his hair and beard, like a dog drying off, and break into a huge, hearty laugh. I will never forget that beautiful laugh. He loved this ritual, and we would do it over and over. It must have felt so good to him.

Don wanted his story to be told because he felt he lived through experiences that might help someone else like him—someone else who could not communicate, who needed care and understanding, and who needed a place to work or live and someone to love him or her.

For someone who was deprived of so many of the things in life that most of us take for granted, Don Fulk truly and genuinely loved life and was an inspiration to those around him.

It was and is an honor to be your interpreter, your mentor, and, most of all, your friend. This book is for you, Don.

Don and Betty with their bridesmaids: Dee (left)
and Janet (the author of this book).

# Where Are They Now?

Betty Anne Fulk, Don's beloved wife. She is very active in the Deaf community and working for the rights of disabled people.

Laurie Fulk Kimball (left) and Val Fulk Kendall. Laurie married in 2011 and now lives in Ventura, California. Val is a retired registered nurse (thirty-five years), living in Olympia, Washington.

Steven, Paul Howard, and Kendall Fulk. Steven is a retired elementary school teacher who lives in Palm Springs, California. Paul Howard (1940–1985) is remembered with love by all the Fulk siblings. Kendall retired after forty-one years of being the owner/operator of Yellow Cab Co.

Kathy Fulk Douglas. She is currently living in Norman, Oklahoma.

Judy Peknik (now Judy Davera Gough). She is retired now and happily married to Ella Mae Lentz. They live in Hayward, California.

George Peknik (1925–1993). He was a mentor and friend to Don as he gained his independence.

Glenna Cooper, MA, ASLTA. She is the department chair and an assistant professor of ASLE at Tulsa Community College in Tulsa, Oklahoma.

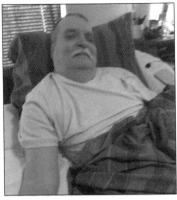

Woody Osburn (1951–2018). He was living independently in his own apartment in Owasso, Oklahoma, and actively working for the rights of people with disabilities.

Kathleen Kleinmann is the executive director of TRIPIL (now TRPIL) in Washington, Pennsylvania.

Gerald Davis (1951–1993). Gerald was named the Vocational Rehabilitation Counselor of the Year because of his work with Don. He, along with Don, is the true hero of this story. He was instrumental in getting Don out of the nursing home and in finding Don a job, as well as leading him to independence.

Connie Foster. She retired from Lowrance Electronics and is now enjoying life and being thankful for her good health.